DANCING
—— in the ——
VALLEY

Finding Life and Joy
Amidst the Shadow of
Death Nipping at My Heels

Rose Booth

PUNCHLINE
PUBLISHERS

All Scripture cited is from the Christian Standard Bible (CSB) unless noted

First edition December 2023

Cover design by C. W. Roederer

ISBN 978-1-955051-24-8 Print
ISBN 978-1-955051-25-5 eBook

Published by Punchline Publishers
www.punchlineagency.com

www.rosebooth.net

Endorsements

— · • ● • · —

"Prolonged suffering can break or make a person. By the strength that only God provides, Rose Booth has allowed God to use suffering to make her into the kind of woman we read about in her life story. Far from allowing her suffering to define her, she uses her suffering to tell the wonderful story of gospel transformation. Read this story, be challenged and encouraged to trust in God more fully and follow Him more faithfully."

—Dr. Bill Cook,
Professor of New Testament Interpretation,
The Southern Baptist Theological Seminary; Lead Pastor,
The Ninth & O Baptist Church; Author of *Victory Over the Enemy*

"Rose Booth is a shining example of godliness and faithfulness to the Lord Jesus Christ. This book is but one more evidence of this truth. Rose has experienced wonderful blessings in her life, but she has also faced and endured many challenges and continues to do so. Her winsome spirit, authentic concern for others, and deep insights pertaining to life serve as words of wisdom and encouragement to everyone who desires to live a life that glorifies Christ in every season of life. Furthermore, Rose's story is an invitation to others to experience the same joy and security she has because of her faith in Christ."

—Dr. T.J. Betts,
Professor of Old Testament Interpretation at
the Southern Baptist Theological Seminary and author of
How to Teach the Old Testament to Christians

Dedication

· •● · ·

To Jesus, my Lord and Savior, who has been near to me since I decided to follow Him and has never left my side.

To my mom and dad. Though you are no longer here on earth, your lives and legacy live on through me. Thank you for never giving up so I could have this life. Until then.

Epigraph

"Remember this, had any other condition been better
for you than the one in which you are, divine love would
have put you there."

Charles Spurgeon

"Your eyes saw me when I was formless;
all my days were written in your book and planned before a
single one of them began."

Psalm 139:16

Table of Contents

— •●• —

Introduction

Chapter One

AUGUST 28, 1964

"The baby is coming. But it's way too early. I'm only five months along." These were the words Rose uttered when she realized the baby she was carrying was on its way, but not the way she expected. Her husband, Floyd, immediately took her to the hospital with mixed emotions of what would happen next. They didn't say much as they arrived at the hospital, expecting the worst but hoping for the best.

After three miscarriages and 17 years of marriage, Rose and Floyd had finally made it to the five-month mark. And now the baby was coming early. Could this really be happening? But it was. After a few hours in labor, a baby was finally born to these two anxiously awaiting a child. A baby boy entered the world. He was born at 11:00 pm at St. Mary's and Elizabeth Hospital in Louisville, Kentucky.

Four hours later, at 3:00 am, he was gone. His cause of death was attributed to prematurity and atelectasis—a collapsed lung. In this day and age of medical technology, he would have lived. But not in 1964. Hopes and dreams were dashed. A couple longing for a child came so close, only to experience loss a fourth time.

As the medical staff completed the final paperwork, a nurse approached Floyd and Rose and asked, "What would you like to name the baby?" Without hesitation, they said, "Floyd H. Booth, Jr." Looking perplexed, the nurse said, "Are you sure?" Emphatically they said, "Yes." Rose responded first and said, "This may be the only child we ever have, and we want to name him after his dad."

The story in the pages to follow tells my story. My name is Rose, but I am not the mother in this tragic tale. I am her daughter. You see, God had other plans for this defeated couple. He had blessings waiting, but in the depth of a wilderness of struggle, this couple had no idea what was in store.

SEPTEMBER 28, 1965

After the loss of my brother following three miscarriages, my parents were discouraged to say the least. Dr. Charles Bryant was my mom's doctor. He was one of those good old-fashioned general doctors who treated the common cold and delivered babies. He sat down with my mom shortly after this loss and said, "Get right back out there and try again." Really? Pretty progressive for 1964, Dr. Bryant. But try they did, and four months later I was conceived.

Because of my parent's trust in God and their doctor, I would enter the world a year and a month after my brother. The weather was starting to turn crisp, much cooler than the year before. The time had come for me to be born. My parents lived with cautious optimism. No baby shower. The crib and highchair were borrowed. During this pregnancy, my mom felt the best she ever had. Her doctor had discovered she was a type 2 diabetic, so his care for her stepped up to ensure this pregnancy would go full term. My due date was October 3, but the doctor decided to induce on September 28 to have more control in case something went awry.

Mom arrived at the same hospital where my brother was born with a bravery I wish I could have seen. She arrived at 8:00 am, and the Pitocin drip began. At 2:00 pm, Mom had her first labor pain. At 4:38 pm, I was born. I was 8 pounds 14 ounces and healthy. Little did she know that this baby would begin a life not only marked by miracles but laced with the unbelievable.

This is my story.

MY STORY

The story I want to share is about how my life has been a mix of miracles and struggles. Triumph and tragedy. Unexplainable, yet intentional, and from the providential Hand of God. To begin, I share about who I am and then take you on a journey through my life, from my first breath until today. I focus on a recent time when my world was turned upside down and I almost left this earth three separate times. But having some background of my story helps show all the pieces at play. My hope is that you will see the weaving of God's miraculous works in the midst of the darkest of days. And how I've been broken and rebuilt by His Mighty Hand, all for His Glory.

From the first moment I can remember, I was told I was a miracle. You've gotten the pretty dismal snapshot of my parents' lives—18 years of marriage, three miscarriages, one premature baby who died shortly after birth. So, when my mom was able to carry me to full term and deliver a healthy baby, that was nothing short of a miracle. I never knew my brother, but somehow his sacrificed life allowed mine to exist. Had he survived, I might not be here. My parents might have had their one child and been content. I often think of my brother and the sacrifice he made without even knowing it. It modeled the gospel for me before I could even comprehend what Jesus did.

My parents were followers of Christ, so I was in church from the moment I hit the cradle roll. I came to follow Him at age eight (more on that later) and live to serve Him to this day. Even though there are plenty of only children, I seem to have been raised differently. My exposure to other only children portrayed an outcome of extremely spoiled and whiny kids, expecting their parents to cater to their every whim. My parents pushed me to be independent and make my own life. They knew how fragile life was and wanted me to develop relationships that would last long after they were gone. Smart cookies.

When I was young, they would frequently remind me that they wouldn't be around for most of my life as they were older, so I needed to make friends that were like family. On more than one holiday, when we'd get home from our festivities, I'd have a friend who'd want to spend time together. Unlike most only-child parents, mine eagerly pushed me to go and enjoy. To them, it was planting seeds of relationships that would last a lifetime.

My parents were always there if I needed advice or help on a decision. After they helped me set up my first bank account as a senior in high school, I can't remember another decision they didn't let me make entirely on my own. From deciding what I would do for college to buying cars, they were there to answer questions, but ensured I was taking the lead. Even though I loved that independence, I was and am still not a fan of adulting.

When someone asks me to share about myself, I typically describe myself like this... I'm a single, never-married woman who loves the Lord. I've worked for thirty-plus years in publishing and technology and am not sure where my next venture will take me (again, more on that later). I am active at my local church, teaching ladies the Bible and co-leading our women's ministry. In my free time, I love to craft, read, and spend time with friends. And I love to write. But you've probably figured that out by now.

As an only child of older parents, I was quite unique growing up. I was the only grandchild on my mom's side of the family. On my dad's side, I was one of a ka-zillion grandchildren but the only one my grandparents never met. My dad was one of eight children, and he was a twin. The first four of his siblings were born, then came some gap years, and then the second four were born. He and his twin brother were in the second set of siblings. Due to my paternal grandparents' older age when my dad was born, and the 18 years my parents waited for me, they both passed before they could meet me. My dad's oldest sister, my Aunt Stella, was like a grandma to me, and we would visit her every summer in Michigan. She and I were pen pals until the day she died. I felt like God gave me a little bit of my grandma in her.

I never had a pet and was obsessed with stuffed animals. I served on the newspaper staff during high school and scored a rare interview with the new county superintendent upon his arrival in the position for a story I was writing. If I'm anything, I'm tenacious.

These are a few glimpses into my life and environment as a child. My young life was different than most with my physical limitations and medical issues. As I grew into my young adult years though, life seemed to level out with some normalcy, but then my life took some twists and turns that would test the strongest of souls. Like most others, I have faced extreme tragedy and loss—near-fatal car accidents, the loss of both of my parents, and recent battles with my health when my life almost ended. My life has been marked by moments where I have watched others, and myself, dance in the valley of death.

You may be thinking, "Rose, how is your story any different than the countless others who've faced tragedy and loss? What's in this book that isn't in the handful of others about tragedy?" I'll answer that question by asking you some questions:

- Do you believe your life has a purpose?
- How do you get through the valleys and struggles of life?
- Is there really a God if you're going through suffering?
- Okay, you believe in God. But does He really love you?

If those questions have ever crossed your mind, driven by tragedy or not, this book is for you. My goal is to show you my journey in all the reality that it has been. No Christian sugar coating. I love Jesus, but traveling this journey called life has not been easy. Maybe you are a believer and say, "I can't rejoice in my suffering." Get on board this train! We'll wrestle together with what it means to live in a broken world and watch God work.

I began following Christ at the young age of eight and grew in my faith, especially during the college years. It was then that I learned how to have true time with the Lord daily and experienced the joy of having other believing friends who challenged and encouraged me. When my life took a turn for the worse in November 2019, I knew the foundation of the faith I had was all I had. I always felt like I'd been through enough in my life and was in a good place spiritually that something so tantamount wouldn't happen to me. Little did I know the battle I would face physically and spiritually.

I can't promise by the end of this book that you'll have all the answers. But I know who does—God. My goal is to point you towards Him and not to give up. Let's go!

THE VALLEY OF THE SHADOW OF DEATH

Psalm 23:4 reads, "Even though I walk through the valley of the shadow of death, I fear no evil; for You are with me. Your rod and Your staff; they comfort me." (NASB) I've read this verse no less than a thousand times, and I have been intrigued by the phrase "the valley of the shadow of death." Christians often interpret that as difficult times, suffering, and that period before we enter into eternity with our Savior.

You may wonder, as did I, if there is an actual valley of the shadow of death. In Israel, there is a place called the Valley of the Shadow of Death. It's known to be a steep, narrow, and dark canyon where the sun only reaches when it's directly overhead. It's thought that David brought his sheep up this valley.[1]

Let's think about the real valley as it relates to what we read in Scripture. David wrote Psalm 23 and used this imagery—as he did with sheep—to show a picture of a tough valley that only saw the sun when it was directly overhead. We know the "Son" —Jesus—is with us as believers no matter where we go in the form of His Holy Spirit. He resides

---

[1] *Life's Dark Valleys*, https://www.thespectrum.com/story/life/features/mesquite/2017/03/03/lifes-dark-valleys/98636638/

"overhead" to guide us through the most difficult passageways in our life, just like the sun is evident in the valley when it is directly overhead. How much more vivid this verse becomes!

In my life, I've watched those I love travel through the valley of the shadow of death. My mom died in 2000, and as she lay in a coma, at one point, she sat up and raised her hands saying, "Daddy, Daddy." Maybe she saw my granddaddy, or maybe she saw her Eternal Father. The Son surely was overhead of her at that moment, and she was ready to go to her heavenly home. I watched my dad suddenly pass in 2013 and know his journey through the valley was short compared to so many.

Multiple times, I have found myself dancing in the valley of the shadow of death. What does that mean? It's a phrase I've used during the times I have danced with death, either personally or in observation of others. The first time I danced in the valley of death was when my family was involved in a car accident when I was seven. This event haunted me because everyone said I shouldn't have survived the accident. A mere change in seating and I probably wouldn't have. So, to me, that's dancing.

Why dancing? That word seems awfully joyful to use for such tragic events. Maybe. But even though I didn't pass from this life to the next, I've been on the cusp. And I see it as dancing because there is nothing I look forward to more than being in Heaven. Now, I only have felt that way after a recent turn of events in my life. I would quote my dad who would say, "Heaven is my home, but I'm not homesick yet." This life is all we know, and we want to make the most of our time here.

Let me remind you, though, this isn't where the real party happens. It happens in Heaven. And there will be dancing. So why not start when we're on our way to that destination?

Being spared in that accident was a miracle and a blessing. I wouldn't truly grasp that until I would dance in the valley again.

The Early Years

Chapter Two

1970

By the age of five, I knew something was not right in my body. My ankles were sore and stiff, and I couldn't walk far without asking my dad to carry me. The pain was unbearable; my ankles had become rigid, unable to move like normal ankles. Oh, I played and romped in the backyard and the kindergarten playground, but walking any distance was out of the question.

That's when my long journey of medical procedures and doctors began. After seeing my general doctor (good ole Dr. Bryant!), he referred us to orthopedic doctors to evaluate me. From ages 5 to 12, I saw more doctors and had more tests than most people do in a lifetime. From brain waves to X-rays, I was poked and prodded endlessly. My mom continued to remind me of the harsh look on my face after my first brain wave. After all the prodding I'd been through, the brain wave was the last straw. During a brain wave, electrodes with small metal discs are affixed to your scalp. I distinctly remember the feeling of the two electrodes on my temples pressing into my head like heavy railroad spikes. When it was done and I was reunited with my mom, my furrowed brow and pouty lip told a story. Your girl here was not happy.

I endured countless appointments, and yet there were no conclusive answers. I had my physical limitations, but I pressed on by the grace of God. Around the age of eight or nine, I was sent to the Child Evaluation Center in my city of Louisville, Kentucky. They ran all sorts of tests, from neurological to behavioral. I spent a good two days going through multiple consultations. The final report was issued to my parents with this highly medical diagnosis: "All indications are normal. The only issue we see is that her body is built like a lemon on two toothpicks."

My parents were livid. Say what? Because my legs were skinny based on the proportion of my torso, doctors assumed this was causing my pain and limitations. My parents were pretty resilient people, but they were getting close to the end of their ever-fraying rope.

The last orthopedic surgeon I saw in 1977 said an expert from Johns Hopkins University would be in Lexington, Kentucky, at the Chandler Medical Center, the hospital associated with the University of Kentucky. He felt having an examination with this expert would be beneficial in targeting my problem. Once again, I was pulled out of school to head to Lexington for a day of evaluation.

I remember exactly what I was wearing that day—a red, white, and blue outfit my mom had just bought me. After this visit, I never wanted to wear it again, mainly due to the memories it conjured up. This visit would be the last one I'd have before moving on with life, still with my pains, and still no answers.

After the day of testing, the team of doctors suggested a muscle biopsy. No one had ever said anything about my muscles. Quite frankly, they were pretty strong compared to my joints. My dad asked, "So if we do this biopsy, will we have answers?" They said, "Not necessarily. There are 40-plus muscle diseases, and we aren't sure that is even the issue, but it's the only thing we think could shed some light." My dad, who was never short on words, said, "We'll pass. I'm not putting her through anything else if we can't be assured of answers."

That was it. The doctors and my orthopedic surgeon told me to live life and if I showed signs of other problems we could investigate further. I was done. Years of learning nothing, yet still suffering, were exhausting. Life continued on, albeit with adaptations. I continued the piano lessons I had started in the second grade and found joy in reading and crafts. Searching for hobbies that were less physically demanding helped me stay busy. I still experienced pain but learned to block it out, and often pushed through it. If I was on a school outing, I would keep walking even though I wanted to cry because my ankles hurt so terribly. I wanted to be a "normal" kid, so part of me was thrilled this journey of constant medical assessments was over, and I fought to ignore the symptoms that persisted despite a lack of answers. It worked for the most part—until 1993. But more on that later.

Hindsight being the 21st century, I was likely suffering from what is now diagnosed as juvenile rheumatoid arthritis (JRA). Though some pediatric arthritis diagnoses occurred overseas long before the 1970s, the first JRA diagnoses in the U.S. came in the late 1970s/early 1980s with more accessible treatment available in the 1990s—too late for me and my childhood pain.

My childhood and adult life were very different due to this journey of suffering. I look back on my life and think, "What if they could have diagnosed and treated me in 1970?" Perhaps my later diagnosis of rheumatoid arthritis (RA) would have been easily diagnosed. Or if I could have received the treatments available for JRA today back in 1970, the outcome of my health might have been different. If my JRA could have been treated, I would have missed out on the life I had, which wasn't all doctors and hospitals. It was marked by slowing down and finding enjoyment in a gentler-paced life. I couldn't hike through the woods or run sprints with my friends. I often found myself on the sidelines watching and cheering others on, but it gave me a perspective on life I might not have ever had. Because of my pain, I became an avid reader. This activity wasn't physically taxing on my body. I also learned to play the piano. My hands didn't suffer from any issues, and keeping them moving up and down the keyboard helped me feel accomplished.

My mom gave me a choice as a young girl—"You can participate in Girl Scouts or take piano lessons, but not both." Given I wasn't the outdoorsy type, I chose piano. Down deep, that was her choice for me, but she did give me the option. My mom had been given a piano when she was younger. Her family could never afford to pay for her to have lessons. It was her dream to one day have a daughter who would play the piano, and though she gave me a choice, I had heard the stories about her childhood piano and knew that was her desire for me all along. I took those lessons for eleven years and ended up teaching beginners piano as my part-time job during college.

Though my physical challenges kept me from playing sports or doing things other girls my age might do, God used this time and the hobbies I *could* do. Piano would later supplement my income and be part of my first ministry position in my local church—playing the piano for children's choirs. Even in the midst of what could have been disappointment, God blessed.

I likely would have never sat still long enough to practice or play the piano if my body would have let me be as active as the next person. To this day, I know I would have found myself competing in some sport and taking a different path. My spirit was driven and competitive but trapped in a body that couldn't be athletic. God used this wilderness of limitations to prepare me for my first role in ministry long before I followed Him as my Savior.

Psalm 16:11 says, "You reveal the path of life to me; in your presence is abundant joy; at your right hand are eternal pleasures." David wrote this psalm and, though we're not sure of the context, he was proclaiming his satisfaction in God. I love the opening verse, which says, "Keep me safe, my God, for in you I take refuge." Oh how God has kept me safe and has been my Refuge...even when I had no idea what He was doing.

When you are in a wilderness and can't see what it means, look through the dust and chaos and see how God is shaping you for something in your future you can't yet see.

Chapter Three

November 5, 1972

———— ·•●•· ————

It was a crisp, sunny Sunday afternoon. When we left church that day, my dad wanted to head to Madison, Indiana. I let out a "harrumph" because my normal Sunday afternoons were usually filled with good food at my granny's house and spending the day with her. As any seven-year-old would do, I whined a bit about why we had to go and couldn't we just spend the day at Granny's. Seven-year-olds don't win in those arguments, at least not in my world.

We headed to the cemetery in Madison to see my grandparents' graves. Spending the day driving to walk around a morbid cemetery to find my Grandma and Grandpa Booths' gravesites was not appealing. Especially given I never met these grandparents, and I preferred being with the granny I did know. But my dad was determined to go, so we all three loaded up and headed north.

This was in the day before car seats and safety regulations. I always sat between my mom and dad in the front seat. Always. I didn't like being in the backseat by myself but preferred to be up where the action was. Bench seats allowed for that to happen, and my parents would oblige. You'll soon find out how life-saving a choice that was for me.

After we visited the cemetery, we headed home. I had my notepad and pencil in hand and was drawing away, oblivious to the world. And then it happened. BOOM. Our car was hit, and we went flying. I don't remember much and likely passed out for part of this event, but when I came to, I was stuck under the glove compartment on the passenger side at my mom's feet. I could hear voices but had no idea what happened. When I was pulled out of the car, I saw giant pigs standing next to the car. Now, they weren't really giant, but to a small child, they seemed giant. I can't remember who pulled me out of the car, but I saw my dad standing there talking to a policeman. The swoosh of cars whizzing by above my head made me realize the powerful hit our car took had caused it to careen over the guardrail and into a field. A field of pigs. I don't know if I was more concerned about being attacked by a giant pig or that something awful had just happened.

There was a lot of commotion, and I saw my dad up and moving, but my mom was on a stretcher. My dad seemed somewhat okay, but my mom, not so much. I remember seeing blood all over the car seat when I was pulled out. Since I didn't notice any blood from me, I knew it must have been from my mom. From what I recall, they wheeled her into the back of the ambulance, and my dad was with her. They plopped me in the front seat with my dad's handkerchief because I was bleeding on the bridge of my nose. I remember the siren being so loud and a piece of glass coming out of the corner of my eye. I tried to hand it to the driver who told me to just hold on to it. What I don't remember, but was told later, is that I asked everyone I saw not to let my mommy die.

After arriving at the hospital, we found out that my mom had broken her pelvic bone in five places. She was eventually transported to a local hospital in Louisville where we lived, and her recovery would be long. She would be in the hospital for weeks before coming home to rehabilitate. This was a serious injury and more than my little mind could comprehend. As an only child and introvert, my mind went into overdrive. This might have been the first time I became an overthinker. All of a sudden, life wasn't the same anymore. My mom wouldn't be taking me to school. I found myself being taken care of by my granny and neighbors while my dad tended to my mom and worked his job. The biggest thought that kept running through my mind was how my mom and dad could have died, and I could have died. I couldn't get my head around the fact that I could have lost my parents. All of a sudden, death became a reality.

My dad wrote letters to my mom in the hospital. This was odd because, yes, he visited her daily, but Dad communicated well in writing and sometimes better than in person. I still have some of those letters he wrote to her during recovery. He would tell her how I was doing and the questions I was asking. This wasn't the only time letters strengthened the bond between my mom and dad. Letter writing was how they fell in love. You see, my mom and dad met while he was serving in the Navy during World War II, so he first learned how to be the most vulnerable with my mom through his letters. Writing to her while she was in the hospital for so long was a healing balm for my dad.

Watching all of these events unfold rocked my world. Our normal life schedule changed and things that I depended on my mom for were being done by my dad and various other people. Going to bed without her there to kiss me goodnight seemed wrong. I was scared that maybe she wouldn't come home. The first time I went to see my mom at the hospital, my granny fixed my hair in two big ponytails with curls. I was scared to death to see her. Would she look the same? Could she hug me? It was so much to take in my seven-year-old mind. Of course, she did look the same and could hug me, so my little heart was calmed. After weeks in the hospital, Mom finally came home. I was overjoyed! She spent a lot of time in a recliner in my room recovering, and I was so happy. Having my mom home somehow gave me the assurance that she wasn't going to die, which became my biggest fear in the weeks following the accident.

As she got back to life and returned to doing what she had always done, I began to show signs of the trauma I experienced from the accident. Every day when she dropped me off at school, I would ask, "Are you going to be back to pick me up after school?" This indicated I knew the fragility of life and maybe she wouldn't be back to pick me up. That was heavy and ominous thinking for a youngster. I lived in fear of death, not only of my parents but even my own death. Things weren't supposed to change this drastically in a young child's life, yet mine felt out of control since the accident. On that Sunday afternoon, my whole world changed, but I was trying desperately to keep things the same and to be assured my mom and dad weren't going to die by the time I got out of school.

What God used from this traumatic incident was what drew me to follow Jesus as my Lord. After the accident, everyone who had been at the scene asked, "How did you all survive that accident?" From what I understood, we were at a stop sign turning left on a two-lane road. To the right, the driver was coming over a hill at an advanced speed and hit us broadside on the passenger side of the car. This was why my mom was severely injured. The impact of the car was so intense, we were catapulted over the guardrail into the field below. I remember my dad feeling guilty for a long time that he didn't see the oncoming driver. According to police, the other driver was going at such a top speed, he likely came on faster than my dad would have seen or realized. Dad and I walked away with scrapes and bruises. Mom, of course, didn't. And it was confirmed that had I been in the backseat, sans car seat (it was 1972), I likely would have been thrown from the car and died. All of this information haunted me as I thought of my family's near experience with death. This was the first time I danced in the valley of the shadow of death.

I had been raised in the church, so I knew enough that if you follow Jesus, you live with Him forever. I knew my parents were believers, and I knew that was a decision they couldn't make for me; I had to make it for myself. However, I hadn't quite connected the dots since I assumed death was for people very much older than me. After the accident and our dance with death, God began to work in my heart to start asking questions about becoming a Christian. The thought of being separated forever from my parents was something I couldn't fathom. I loved Jesus, but I was just learning what following Him and asking Him into my life meant. For as long as I could remember, I heard about Jesus. I knew He loved me, but the concept of being a follower of Jesus was something I hadn't really considered until I came so close to death and being separated from Him for eternity.

In August of 1973, an evangelist named Angel Martinez came to my church, Ninth & O Baptist Church—the church I still attend to this day. In the 1970s, evangelists were having revivals at Baptist churches all the time. One thing Angel Martinez did was make the gospel so simple, even a child could understand. He shared how to pray to receive Jesus as your Savior. My mom said she saw me praying along with Angel Martinez to accept Christ as my Savior. My head was bowed, and I wasn't playing with my toys, but paying attention. When I raised my head, she said she'd never forget the glow on my face.

Though my mom witnessed that moment, she wanted me to initiate the conversations and truly be sure I was ready to make that commitment in my life. Over the coming months, I started asking questions, and my parents became intentional in answering them. My parents were keen on any conversation that led to questions about faith. I don't remember all the things I asked, but I'm sure I asked about what it meant to follow Jesus and other elementary questions that a seven-year-old would have. We talked about the next steps in my journey of faith, like baptism—which was my biggest fear. I didn't know how to swim and was afraid of drowning, but I knew my first act of obedience was baptism, and I wasn't so sure about that.

After talks with my parents, and then talks with our pastor, I decided to make my commitment public on Sunday, May 12, 1974, which happened to be Mother's Day. Interestingly, my dad had been saved on Mother's Day years before.

I don't remember a thing the pastor preached, but I do remember what I was wearing. It was a green dress that my granny had made, and it became my favorite dress. Unlike my red, white, and blue ensemble from my earlier experiences, I had fantastic memories associated with this outfit. I was ready for the invitation at the end of the sermon so that we could get the show on the road! When the invitation happened, I headed forward and prayed with my pastor to ensure all was settled in my heart. I'm nothing if not thorough, even at age eight.

It was another few weeks before I was baptized. Nothing like the Lord testing your faith out of the gate. The baptism went fine, and I didn't drown. I was so happy after that event—for my salvation and that my first step of obedience went well!

For a long time, I thought my salvation testimony was rather boring. Raised in the church. Saved at the age of eight. But God revealed to me later in life how my testimony was special. I saw God in that horrific car accident. As a young child, I didn't see the significance in the timing and outcome of that event, but God used it to show me how easily life can end and my need to follow Christ at an early age. I don't know if I would have accepted Christ at such a young age had it not been for that accident. Can you be thankful for such a terrible event? In retrospect, I was.

In the story of Noah, he was chastised and made fun of for building that ark when there had been no rain yet. I often ponder how he felt every time someone questioned him, yet he continued on with the task God gave him. What a faithful trooper! Because of his faithfulness, he and his family were saved. While he was gathering gopher wood, he may not have seen God in the midst of his every day. Oh sure, he was following the direction of God on building the ark, but he had to battle the opposition daily from those who thought he was losing his mind. God was working even though others couldn't see it...and I suspect on some days when Noah couldn't see it either.

As life-changing as that accident was, I didn't come to be thankful for it until much later in life when God revealed His presence through that storm. When it all clicked, I was blown away that God would love me enough to save me. Jesus came for me. Jesus died for me. And He preserved my life that day so that I could follow Him.

Only God works in ways that make no human sense.

A ROSE IN BLOOM

Chapter Four

School Life

From my previous chapters, you've learned about how my young life advanced from accepting Jesus to beginning my life of following Him and the medical challenges I experienced as a child. Around the time I was finishing elementary school, the constant parade of medical professionals came to a halt. I was an anomaly of undiagnosable issues but determined to march on with life, defying all odds.

Back in the good old days, elementary school was first through sixth grade, and I loved every minute of my time at Gutermuth Elementary. Our principal, Mr. Downing, had just retired at the end of my fifth-grade year. He and his wife, Juanita, were members of my church and long-time friends of my parents. After my first bout of medical issues, my mom was so concerned about me being able to climb the stairs of our school's two-story building. Mr. Downing promised he would carry me to class if he had to, but I was able to navigate just fine. As principal, Mr. Downing always let the sixth graders come to school barefoot one day before the end of the year, but with the new principal, our dreams were dashed. Our new principal did away with that tradition. The sixth-grade trip remained intact, though. Sixth graders always made a trek to Mammoth Cave, Kentucky. Given my physical limitations, I went on the trip but didn't go on the historic tour that included rough terrain and a climb of 440 stairs to exit. While they were on the tour, I spent my time watching videos of the cave and visiting the gift shop. I felt pretty important and mature since I was entrusted to do all of this by myself.

Leaving elementary school meant attending a much bigger school where I was a small fish in a big pond. I would attend junior high at Doss High School. I had grown up dreaming of being a Doss Dragon. Graduating from Doss High School after spending six years there as a student was what everyone in my part of Louisville aspired to do. I couldn't wait to chant, "Stop, look, and listen, here come the mighty dragons!" It was all I could have hoped for, and I felt all grown up with my days of haunting medical issues behind me. Many of my elementary school friends joined me at Doss, but I also made a lot of new friends. One of my best friends was Monique. We hit it off in homeroom, and the rest was history.

While I was at Doss in junior high, my parents applied for me to attend a traditional public school. These schools were more stringent on discipline and college preparatory classes. At the time, there was only one traditional middle school/junior high and one traditional high school. I had been accepted and could have gone in eighth grade, but opted to stay at Doss to finish junior high. My dream of being a Doss Dragon would only last for two years as I would be headed to Male High School as a freshman. Doss had both junior and senior high, but Male was strictly a high school. I was sad about leaving, but due to the current school assignments, unless I was in the traditional school, I wouldn't be able to spend all four years of high school at one school. In those days, we had school assignments to integrate our student population based on the first letter of our last name. I could have attended Doss through 10th grade but would then have had to transfer to another high school for my junior and senior years—the most exciting two years of high school. To me and my parents, spending all four years at one high school was more important. Going to Male Traditional High School was the best option.

One morning close to the end of our eighth-grade year, Monique was lamenting over having to change schools, and we soon discovered that we were both going to Male! What a joyous day that was to know that one of my best friends would be with me in high school! Going to a new school, no matter how much I wanted to, was scary. But now, with my best friend going, I knew it wouldn't be as frightful.

In the fall of 1979, I was a high school freshman. My nerves got the best of me the night before as I prepared to get up early to catch the first school bus of my life. I could hardly sleep, as if the next morning I was going to walk a tightrope across the Grand Canyon. Since my first day of kindergarten, my mom always took me to school. Because Male was downtown, it was time for me to be a big girl and ride the bus. At 6:30 am, I caught my bus and went to begin my first day of high school. Male was a three-story building, but I was able to travel up and down the steps with minor issues. The confidence I gained in being able to function as a normal teenager at school was immense. I still had periodic pain in my joints, but I did my best to ignore it and enjoy this life I had.

My high school years brought me out of my shell as I became the jokester on the bus rides and ended up on the newspaper staff in my junior and senior years. I was far from the popular girl in my class, but I had a wide range of friends and often thought, "This is what high school is supposed to feel like." Even though my high school years were as close to "normal" as I could have hoped, I still experienced that dance in the valley.

In January 1980, my freshman year, my Uncle Bill died suddenly of a heart attack at age 40. He was my mom's only brother and much like a second dad to me. He and my Aunt Mary never had children, but they did have a beautiful collie named Crystal. She was my pride and joy. I never owned a dog as a child, but Crystal was mine. Many an afternoon, I would take naps on the bed, cuddled up with her. I had always been told that if my parents both died, my aunt and uncle would raise me. That carried a lot more meaning, given the close call of that becoming a reality after our accident in 1972.

My mom got the call late one Wednesday night when I was already in bed. I heard the commotion and woke up to hear her tell my dad, "My brother is dead." I shook my head as if to wake myself up from a bad dream and realized this wasn't a dream—this was reality. My stomach felt like it was doing flips. I didn't get out of bed but just laid there so I could process alone.

The next few days were horrible as an autopsy was done to discover the cause of death and the visitation and funeral were set. I felt numb. Both my Aunt Mary and my granny were basketcases. I didn't say much to anyone because I didn't know what to say. This was the first time I'd experienced the death of someone I was so close to, and I didn't know how to act or feel, so I just observed. I'll never forget sitting in the front row of the funeral. I couldn't look at my uncle in the casket. He looked like he was sleeping, not dead. They played "How Great Thou Art," and for years after, I couldn't listen to that song. My memories of almost losing my parents were called back from my mind. This time around, I had the assurance that I would be with Jesus when I died, but dancing in this valley with someone else's death was hard.

The valley would continue to present itself in my life in the coming years. In January 1981 and January 1982, I lost my granddaddy and then my Aunt Stella, my dad's oldest sister. Those were blows as well since my granddaddy was the only grandfather I had. When he would visit us from the country, he always took a walk with me around the block. Being older, we'd have to stop and rest on a concrete slab, which was great for me because just about the time we stopped was when my ankles were hurting. My granddaddy was an eloquent writer, which is where I got my writing gene from. My Aunt Stella was like a grandmother to me. Since I never knew my Grandma Booth, she was the stand-in for that role in my life. She lived in Michigan, and we were pen pals since the moment I could write coherently. My family visited her every summer, and she'd plan out our week based on things I wanted to do that she had done throughout the year. Losing both of them back-to-back after my uncle's death kept one foot in the valley. Thankfully, my senior year, was free from any death, for which I was thankful.

After high school, I attended Sullivan University, a local college, to obtain an associate degree in business administration. Deciding on college was a challenging decision. I really didn't know what I wanted to do, although something business-related was appealing. My dad was given the option for early retirement when I was a senior in high school, so I didn't want to burden my parents with school costs. I knew too many people who graduated with a four-year degree who were working a retail job. I wanted to go to a school that would equip me to go to work and help me find a job. Sullivan was the best option. Once I decided on my pathway, I applied for scholarships and got a full scholarship to attend Sullivan. That was a blessing from the Lord.

Once again, I was heading into unfamiliar waters. All of my friends headed off to school at the University of Louisville, Bellarmine University, or the University of Kentucky. Monique went to Eastern Kentucky University, and we kept up with each other's lives via letters. (Remember, this was pre-internet days).

I graduated and landed a job at an automotive dealership as a sales support administrative assistant. Later in my career, I went back to get my bachelor's degree in business administration, with a concentration in accounting and marketing from Sullivan University. That might sound like a weird combination, but I started out with only a concentration in accounting. I took a marketing class and fell in love. So, with just four more classes, I could do a double concentration to include marketing. It took me a few years to finish as I continued working full-time, but I completed my degree in 1998.

Shortly before my dad passed away in 2013, I felt the urge to go back to school for my MBA. I waffled on my decision and, after research, chose to apply to Campbellsville University. The tuition was cost-effective, and I could do the entire degree online. My dad passed the beginning of May 2013, and I was scheduled to sit for the GMAT at the end of May to fulfill my last qualification for entrance to the MBA program. Motivated by my dad's pride, I pushed through with flying colors and spent the next two years finishing my MBA, graduating in 2015. Even when I danced in the valley, I used it to propel me through studying for my MBA and working full-time, managing a staff of eleven employees.

My friend, Monique, graduated from Eastern Kentucky University with an education degree and began teaching elementary school. She married her love, Joe, in 1987, and I was privileged to be part of the musical group that performed at their wedding. Monique made sure our group of friends got together every summer and always at Christmas. She was the ringleader of our friends.

In 1991, Monique became pregnant, and we were all excited for her and Joe. While on a camping trip with some of our friends, she went into labor when she was just five months along. After being rushed to the hospital, she delivered a little girl, Sara Marie. They both battled for their lives in the wake of the early delivery. When they took little Sara, they found that Monique had a rare disease that was causing her internal organs to disintegrate like wet tissue paper. Later it would be discovered that she contracted this disease after being born on an army post in Germany. Neither she nor Sara lived.

I got word of her death while I was at work. A co-worker was a close friend of the family, and he came into my office and got down on one knee at my desk to break the news. I was in shock. I couldn't cry because I was processing this unbelievable news. We would soon have been planning Monique's baby shower. This isn't how this was supposed to go. I danced in the valley again, trying to understand how and why my friend and her baby had left this earth far too soon.

Mustering up all the courage I had, I went to the visitation. There she was in the casket, holding baby Sara. It was a nightmare. Her mom hugged me and said, "This now all makes sense, Rose." Monique had odd health issues throughout high school—terrible migraines, losing her eyesight, getting sick frequently—and no one could figure out why. Now, all of these symptoms made sense as the rare disease was at work in her body all along. The pregnancy brought it on quicker, but doctors explained that she likely wouldn't have lived past her 30s.

Monique and Sara's funeral might have been one of the saddest funerals I've ever attended. And we know that I've been to my fair share just in my own family. I went alone, as I wanted it that way to grieve this loss by myself. As I sat in the pew, taking deep breaths, I just wanted it to be all a dream. But it wasn't.

Monique was Catholic and had a full mass funeral. As the pallbearers wheeled her casket down the aisle with the priest swinging the incense, I broke down in tears. The last time I was in that church, Monique was walking down the aisle to marry Joe; now she was proceeding down the aisle in a casket. Sometimes life doesn't make sense. I prayed for the family and asked God to forgive me for not more boldly sharing the gospel with Monique. I'm not sure if she was a believer or not, though we had a couple of conversations about our faith.

That dance in the valley taught me once again of the brevity of life, but more importantly, I was reminded of my responsibility to share the truth of the gospel any chance I could get. A seed had been planted to help grow my courage to share the gospel more boldly later in life.

Chapter Five

Work Life

———— ·•●•· ————

Graduating from Sullivan University allowed me an opportunity to participate in their job placement program. The school worked in conjunction with many businesses in my town and helped recent graduates and alumni find jobs. I prepared my resume and went on a few interviews before I finally landed a position with a local automotive dealership, Montgomery Chevrolet, as their sales support administrative assistant.

Fresh out of college at the young age of 19, I started full-time work on December 27, 1984, in an environment that wasn't for the young and naive. Surrounded by salesmen and mechanics, this young, innocent girl was baptized by fire into the real world of blue-collar work. I had become more outgoing in high school but still led a pretty sheltered life. At my new job, I witnessed people from all backgrounds of life. Even though my shock factor dwindled, I loved every minute of working there.

I soon became friends with my office co-workers. From the sales staff to the service and parts staff, everyone became like family. I would spend time on the weekends with co-workers and even dated a couple of employees during my tenure. I moved from my first position there to become the accounts payable clerk and then to assistant office manager. In that role, I administered payroll and assisted the office manager with all back office responsibilities. I worked many hours every week and on the weekends. When a business is open seven days a week, there is always something that has to be done.

It became evident to me that, though I loved the people and what I did there, I had to make a change. The pay and benefits were minimal, and I didn't see that changing soon, along with the hours I was putting in each week. I confided in one of my older co-workers who wisely advised me to get out now or I'd be here for my lifetime. She had worked in automotive dealerships for more than 30 years.

After an updated resume was complete, I began my search and landed a job at The Cobb Group, a technology publishing company, as an accounts payable clerk. After my resignation, my final day of employment at the dealership came and I was showered with so many wonderful gifts and even a dozen roses. It made leaving there even more difficult. I'll never forget when I drove away from work that day and cried all the way home. This place had been my security for seven years. Could I make it at a new place? What if I had made a mistake? I felt a bit of regret but my logical side kicked in reminding me this was the best thing for me.

On September 30, 1991, I started my new job at The Cobb Group. It was a stark contrast from my last job. The environment was more professional with cubicles and offices. It was a technology publishing company, so I was surrounded by super smart techie types who were creative and great writers. Even though I worked in the accounting group, my innovative juices were flowing every day. The company was progressive for the early 90s and had a laid-back dress code that allowed for jeans and shorts and regular opportunities for camaraderie among the employees.

It wasn't long before I knew I had made the right decision. I grew in that company and took on a human resources role along with my accounting responsibilities. There were many opportunities to learn from all departments, so I made friends with co-workers throughout the company. There were a lot of musically talented folks, so I spent a lot of time after hours listening to live music performed by Cobbers (our name for the employees). It was Camelot. The company couldn't have been better, from the unity among the staff to the management leadership; it was definitely a dream place to work.

In 1998, the dream came to an end. Our parent company decided to relocate our office to Rochester, New York. There were rumblings of changes coming, but none of us expected this move to be the outcome. Each employee was presented with a package to relocate to Rochester and keep their job. If we chose not to accept the position, we would be given a severance package. Who wanted to move to Rochester in 1998 when the unemployment rate there was 13% and in Louisville it was 3%? Not to mention, the weather in Rochester was snowy and dreary six months out of the year.

In the end, only three people opted to move with the company. The rest of us took the severance package and began to prepare our resumes. Our parent company was gracious enough to provide outplacement services for free and group grief counseling. For those of us that had been with the company for a while—I'd been there seven years—we had seen our dream crash and were struggling with losing our job and losing a family.

While I was still employed, Kim, a former senior leader of The Cobb Group, contacted me. She and some other previous leaders were in the process of building a new company, and she wanted to bring me on board. They were working on funding, so it would be a few months before I would be given an offer, but given my length of service, my severance package would get me through. I explained that I was finishing up my bachelor's degree and wanted to pursue something in the marketing space. She assured me that if I helped her build the accounting department, she would help me move into that area in the new company. It was one of the best calls of my life. Kim was the person who hired me at The Cobb Group originally, and I trusted her completely.

My last day of employment at The Cobb Group was April 30, 1998, and I enjoyed a summer off as I waited for the call to start my new job at Kim's company, TechRepublic. On September 14, 1998, I began working as an accounting assistant side-by-side with Kim. It was a fun time being part of building a company. The entrepreneurial spirit was quickly sparked in my soul. There isn't anything quite like being a pilgrim in uncharted waters as you set up processes and roles for a brand-new company. TechRepublic was a technology publisher similar to The Cobb Group but all on the internet.

As promised, after the company got rolling, I changed roles and became a marketing and public relations specialist. I was under the tutelage of Barbara, my boss, who was a seasoned marketer. I soaked up all I could learn from her, and it felt like I'd found my calling. From communications to event planning and everything in between, I was in my lane. I enjoyed the detail that accounting provided, but this new role unleashed the creative in me that I didn't know existed. The days were long, but I began to be a part of business lunches and dinners and felt like I had finally arrived.

Our company was partially acquired to allow us the funding we needed to continue growing. What started as ten to fifteen had grown to nearly 100 employees strong. My job duties changed along the way as my expertise was uncovered, and the projects on my plate were invigorating.

Shortly after that acquisition, the acquiring company sold us off to a new company, causing a huge onslaught of layoffs. In April 2001, I was laid off along with all of the founding employees. It was a new day, so the old regime had to go. Much like my last job loss, I received a call from a former co-worker at TechRepublic. He was now a manager at a company called Vobix. He was looking for a marketing communications specialist and thought I'd be fantastic. I submitted my resume, and before April was over, I was hired.

Vobix had a much similar vibe to The Cobb Group and TechRepublic. Our president was a former Cobber, so it had a lot of familiarity. We were owned by ManTech, the largest government contractor in the United States. During this time, many non-technology companies were looking for companies to fund and own. Vobix had multiple arms of business, including working with ISPs (Internet Service Providers), Microsoft Service Providers, and educational institutions. Let's keep it simple to avoid making your eyes gloss over: Vobix helped each of these organizations grow their business through channel marketing.

Five months after I joined the company, September 11, 2001, happened. What a horrible day for our country. As we all tried to get through the coming days, our company began to see the writing on the wall. Our owner, ManTech, would have to focus entirely on the impending war. What did that mean for us? It meant that in March 2002, our company was shut down. ManTech had sold off our clients to competitors, and the doors were closed. This was getting to be a pattern in my career. Even though most people would think I'd change industries or careers, I loved what I did so much that I was willing to take the risks that came with the field.

Thankfully, since I had severance tucked away in savings due to returning to work so quickly, I could make it for a while. My mom had passed away in 2000, and my dad had begun dating. Around the time I lost my job at Vobix, he announced he was getting remarried. As I've done in every shocking situation in my life, I took it like a champ. Then when I went to bed, I cried at all the changes happening in my life. My mom was gone. I had just lost my job...again. My dad was getting remarried. What next?

I went without a job for eight months. Between my severance and unemployment, I was able to make it. I was enjoying my summer off and continued to apply for jobs. By the time fall rolled around, I was ready to get back to work. When the beginning of the holiday season started in November, I feared I'd have to wait until the new year before hiring would pick back up again. This wasn't a time I wanted to ask my dad for financial help, so I prayed that the Lord would sustain me. And He did.

In November 2002, I heard from my first boss at The Cobb Group, Jackie. She was now working for a company called KiZAN as their CFO. It had been started by a Cobber (actually, the same one who had been the president of Vobix), and they were a Microsoft Certified Provider of infrastructure and development services, along with certification training. Jackie was in need of an all-around office manager as her current person was moving. In an answer to prayer at 11:59 pm, I gladly accepted the position. It was a significant pay cut from what I was earning at Vobix, but I needed a job and decided this was best.

KiZAN's environment and team were very similar to my previous jobs, and I quickly felt at home. Not long after being there, a consultant was brought on to make sure the company and employees were properly aligned to generate the most business. His name was Bruce. Though I needed a job, I missed doing the marketing and communications I had done in the past. I felt my creativity dying on the vine. Bruce came in and interviewed each employee. He took that information and proposed some changes. One of those changes was to carve out time for me to work on the marketing side of the business, which was almost non-existent. Another change was to take one of our engineers, Robert, and get him more involved in the business side of the company. Bruce had a keen sense that Robert was also sorely underutilized. I'm happy to report as of 2023, Robert is their CEO.

I spent a lot of time with Bruce, and we went to client meetings and our Cincinnati office so that I could start getting a grasp of what we were doing and what we needed to do in the marketing sphere. With his voice in the CEO's ear, I was able to spread my marketing wings. I remember a specific time, though, when I knew this would be a tough assignment. I had a meeting with the CEO to present various ideas on how we could market more aggressively to gain business. He wasn't 100% on board. I felt dejected but didn't give up as I knew Bruce would be my cheerleader in the background.

A very sad day came when Bruce was diagnosed with lung cancer. He was an avid smoker, and I experienced it as I traveled up and down the highway between Louisville and Cincinnati with him. Unfortunately, Bruce had to step away from consulting to focus on his health. With his leaving, my dream died. I no longer had someone to root for me and stand up for me and the changes I wanted to bring to KiZAN.

Despite this, I wanted to stick it out at KiZAN simply for stability. I wasn't happy with the direction my career was going, but I adored my work family. Exchanging happiness for a consistent job and paycheck seemed the smart thing to do. I put out a feeler to my former Cobb

Group/TechRepublic connections, but I didn't aggressively start to look for a job.

Not long after, I received a call from Tom, a former sales manager at Montgomery Chevrolet, my very first job. He had since become a State Farm agent and was looking for an employee to join his agency. Tom sold the position like a shiny, new car. He would pay for me to get my licenses in property and casualty insurance and health and life insurance and would train me to one day become the office manager. Tom used the angle of getting out of the unstable world of technology and planting myself in an industry that wouldn't be going anywhere. We met up to chat, and after some negotiation of my salary, I decided to take the job in March 2004.

As I look back on this time, I didn't give this decision much prayer. I saw this as an opportunity that came knocking, and I couldn't refuse if the price was right. The former job offers that plopped in my lap weren't always bathed in prayer at the level they should have been. I believed if God opened a door and it seemed the right fit, then it was a blessing from Him. I don't doubt or regret any of my job moves, but this one seemed radical.

I spent a week in Lexington at the property and casualty classes and then began work. I would get my health and life insurance license a few weeks after I started. I couldn't make sales calls until I had my licenses, so I spent most of the day studying and making the daily bank and mail run.

The office consisted of Tom and two other office workers. Dodie was the office manager and Sally was another agent working in a similar position as me. This environment was a complete change for me. I had an office where I could make calls while the other two were in the front office. I had been primarily used to working around men my whole life, so this female-driven dynamic was new. I became the person each woman came to in order to complain about the other one. Soon after I obtained my licenses, Sally told me she was leaving. Once she did, I was moved to the front office reception area to work within a few feet of Dodie.

Tom was rarely in the office, so it was just me and Dodie every day. She wasn't the most positive person on the planet, and I tried my best to be an encouragement, but it didn't always work. I learned a lot about sales, which would serve me well later, but the lack of challenging work was killing my brain cells. Every day was the same. I would arrive at 8:30 am and start the day. By around 9:00 am, I was caught up on emails and had nothing to do unless the phone rang. I couldn't wait until noon when I would get my lunch to eat. Something to do! Then I would watch the clock until 2:30 pm, when I would make the deposit and have the privilege of breaking free to go to the bank and the post office. I would return and watch the clock until 5:00 pm. Every. Single. Day.

At this point, I was bored out of my mind, but I battled with the stability of this industry versus being challenged at my job. I had a perfect 8:30-5:00 day, Monday through Friday. No weekends or overtime like I'd had in previous jobs. Everyone always needed insurance, so there was no threat of business dying off. But I missed my old life. It might have been rocky, but it was invigorating.

During my time at State Farm, I did gain valuable lessons in sales, which would benefit me in the jobs to come. Though there were benefits, my heart was not in this career for the long haul. I kept plodding on, thinking it was the responsible thing to do. Then I was contacted by Kim once again.

She and the team from TechRepublic were gearing up to launch another business—IT Business Edge. They wanted to pull me into the band, so she and I met for dinner, and I was more than intrigued by this possibility. The role would be in marketing, and I'd be a Jacqueline-of-all-trades, which suited me perfectly. My brain cells were dying, and if I didn't get challenged soon, I would forget how to be creative.

Shortly after Kim discussed this opportunity with me, I met with Ken, the VP of sales, and Phil, the president, both of whom I had worked with at TechRepublic. They grilled me pretty hard on my thoughts and ideas. It was thrilling to put my marketing chops to work after being sequestered in a small office calling people to sell an insurance policy.

I agreed to join IT Business Edge and left State Farm in April 2005. What a ride! It wasn't long after joining that I felt like I was driving in a car I had parked in a garage for a year. During my time at State Farm, the Pixar movie *The Incredibles* was released. The story of Mr. Incredible's life as a superhero being minimized to a lowly insurance claims representative was eerily similar to working in technology and then being transported to a small desk doing menial insurance work. He became my inspiration, and as I got into my new position with IT Business Edge, I felt like Mr. Incredible fighting crime again.

Working to help IT Business Edge grow was very similar to the glory days at The Cobb Group. In layman's terms, our company helped technology vendors like IBM and HP generate leads for their solutions. My role evolved, and I ran a test summer program to determine if we could sustain an inside sales team. My sales experience definitely weighed heavily here as I tested through two summer interns whether we could be profitable with an inside sales team. All indicators were pointing to yes, and I was tasked with managing not only our growing sales support team but also an inside sales team.

In August 2011, as I was managing a sales support team, inside sales team, and business development team, IT Business Edge was acquired by QuinStreet. Needless to say, the sound of "acquisition" made me realize I would likely not be here for long as, like other acquisitions, this one came with layoffs. But, unlike every other acquisition in my life, I made it over the line. There is something to be said about survivor's guilt. I spent a lot of my days keeping my team, or what was left of them, upbeat. We were all doing the same thing but trying to fit our business in QuinStreet's bigger infrastructure.

I grew at QuinStreet more than I had grown at any other time in my career. My roles changed and evolved, and this became the last full-time job I had before my health battle would begin. I had advanced to the director level and managed a team of eleven people. My team consisted of sales support and junior sales reps, and I created a summer sales intern program that I led each year. Nothing gave me more joy than training fresh-out-of-college kids to be successful. My duties also included budgeting, forecasting, and month-end closings, hailing me back to my early days.

The Lord has been so faithful throughout my thirty-plus-year business career. I started out in sales support and came full circle, managing a sales support team. No matter how many twists and turns my career took, it all seemed very intentional. He provided for my needs when I had no job. He always took me to better places, even if it didn't seem that way at first. The story of my work life is a testimony of the faithfulness of God.

Chapter Six

Church Life

··•●•··

After accepting Jesus and following Him, I continued to grow at Ninth & O Baptist Church. I was involved in the youth group, though you would find me on the sidelines as a quiet person. I couldn't be as physically active as a normal teenager, but I found myself befriending those in our youth group that were shunned or too quiet to make their own friends. God used me even though I didn't realize it at the time. During my teenage years, I took on my first serving role—playing piano for the children's choirs. That was nerve-wracking but fun and prepared me to lead preschool choirs in the future.

When I moved into the college group, I felt restless. I wanted to be serving or doing something other than hanging with 40 people who seemed much cooler than me. I began to pray about it and felt a calling to teach children in Sunday school. My mom had done that all her life. After working with children's choirs, I also felt like I could serve Him well in that area of ministry. As the Lord would ordain it, our children's director contacted me to ask if I'd be willing to pray about teaching. I told her that I would, even though, in my mind, I knew this call was from the Lord. After a few days, I called her back and said yes.

My first teaching role was sixth-grade girls. I loved it! The first Sunday, though, I was nervous. My dad, who was also a gifted teacher of adults, gave me a pep talk prior to my first Sunday. As it is with most curriculum for children, the new year starts in Genesis. As I pulled out my flannel board to tell the story of creation, I was hit with my first question, and it was a doozy. "Miss Rose, were the animals God created baby animals or adult animals?" Nothing like a question coming out of left field that I was completely unprepared to answer. I did what teachers are taught to do when they don't know an answer. I said, "You know, that's a great question. Let me research that and let you know next week." My research consisted of going home and asking my dad. He was a Bible scholar, so I trusted him. I will never forget his response. "Well, the Bible doesn't tell us, but the Bible does tell us that one of the reasons Adam and Eve were created was to procreate the earth, so it's a strong possibility that the animals were created to do the same and in turn would need to be adult animals." Next week, I went to Sunday school armed with a brilliant answer and the student seemed to be satisfied. No further questions, Your Honor.

I taught sixth-grade girls for another few years before moving to teach second grade alongside my mom. That is a blessing I treasure to this day. To sit under her teaching of little souls that were the age I was when I first began to realize the gospel was for me, was such a gift. Although I loved teaching, I was missing a peer group at church. I was content in my role of service and really didn't realize what I was missing.

A dear friend of mine, Alisa, was a few years older than me. She was constantly inviting me to singles events and to fellowship with them. My introverted heart continued to say, "No thank you, but thanks for asking," over and over again. After her continual berating (in a very kind way), I finally said yes. I joined them for an evening—part of me was curious, and part of me wanted to do this to get her off my back so I could go back to my quiet life. What happened was not exactly what I expected. After my first night with the group, I had found my people! That night was full of fun that I hadn't experienced in ages…if ever. I'd never been the popular girl at church and didn't want to be. But I never had a group of friends that I wasn't "friending" to minister to and not necessarily getting filled up in return. Friendship for me was mostly withdrawals with no deposits. This group was different, and it was in this group that I began to blossom into myself.

After continuing to teach in the children's ministry a while longer, I eventually felt the need to go to my own age group's Sunday school class as I needed the spiritual growth and accountability. I began attending the singles class and growing in the Lord alongside my people. In exchange for teaching children, I joined the adult choir, and music became my new ministry.

In the 1990s, we brought on a new worship pastor, Michael Smith. Not *the* Michael Smith, but definitely equally as talented. He was ahead of his time and recruited a worship team from our choir to begin leading in our services. I was one of those who was chosen, along with Christie, who became one of my best friends. Michael was the first person who taught me what it meant to be a true worship leader, and I admired him so much.

In the late 1990s and the year 2000, our church went through some rocky days. Michael had left, but I still remained in the choir and worship team. It was a difficult time for our congregation. We dwindled down to 150 in attendance at a church that historically had seen 1,000 in attendance and a youth group the size of a small church. There were days I didn't know if our church would survive, but by the grace of God, we did.

Our new pastor, Bill Cook, came in 2001, and the impact of his ministry to our church and to me personally and spiritually could fill a book. Along with him came his family, including his wife, Jaylynn, someone I still count as a best friend. After my mom's passing in 2000, I felt a very strong desire to disciple women. Losing my mom when I was 35 made me realize what a treasure I had. A godly mother who taught me how to grow spiritually was something many women did not have.

Shortly after my mom's passing, I began mentoring and discipling Amber. She was a younger single at our church and was such a joy in my life. You'll hear a lot about her and Jaylynn throughout this book. I was learning the ropes of what it meant to disciple and mentor, and she was patient and kind as we navigated this new thing together. She forever helped me shape my passion into a reality.

Not long after I began mentoring Amber, I was asked by Amy, the leader of our women's discipleship on Wednesday evenings, to lead our women's Bible study. What an honor! I was nervous but excited to use my gifts to teach other women. Amy was the catalyst for my role in women's ministry, even today.

Life in discipleship continued to blossom for me. I was discipling upwards of two to three girls at a time and teaching women on Wednesday nights. My plate and heart were full. I had to make a tough decision, though. I was still active in our worship ministry, both in the choir and worship team, but with working full-time, something had to give. I made the choice to walk away from worship ministry to devote more time to discipleship. Outside of teaching children, music had been my main ministry in recent years. Music had been a part of my life since I was a young girl playing the piano and was a way I connected with God and ministered to others. I didn't take the decision lightly and prayed about it for quite some time. But ultimately, I felt at peace with the decision.

After I had my focus completely on discipleship, I was approached by Jessica, who led our women's ministry. I adored her and her husband, Barry. They had become great friends. She was expecting her first child and wanted help leading and growing our women's ministry. I was honored and humbled to serve alongside her and saw this as a validation from the Lord that my decision to focus on discipleship was the right move.

I am still co-leading our women's ministry today, but now with Jaylynn and my friend Beth. I find so much joy in ministering to the women of Ninth & O Baptist Church. I also co-teach my ladies' Sunday school class, which we call BFG (Bible Fellowship Group), and they have become even more precious to me than I can articulate.

At the time of this writing, I have added to my list of ministry service, helping with the overall discipleship for our church and assisting with our social media strategy. After following Jesus, it took me some time to grow in Him, but my heart has always wanted to serve Him since that day. I pray I'll be serving Him faithfully until my final breath.

LIFE IS NEVER EASY

Chapter Seven

February 1993

It was a cold and blustery morning in February 1993. I was 27 years old and working at The Cobb Group. We'd recently had snow, and the parking lots were still speckled with ice patches. I headed to work one morning and arrived at the office. On my trek in the door, I slipped on one of those random patches of ice. My agility was able to catch me before falling, but I still felt something catch in my left hip.

Over the coming days, it became worse. My hip felt stiff and painful. The echoes of those doctors way back in the 1970s started haunting me. "Live life unless something changes" seemed to be coming to fruition. After suffering from the pain for as long as I could stand it, I made an appointment with my mom's orthopedic surgeon, Dr. Nehill.

It was daunting to be going through all of this again; I felt all those memories of doctors, hospitals, tests, and no answers come flooding back. The doctor did X-rays and sat down to talk with my mom and me. He said I needed a hip replacement, but at 27, he wouldn't do it. Huh? He told me he didn't like doing them until someone was at least 40 so the replacement would last longer.

Being hit with the thought that I would have to live with this pain for 13 more years was unbearable. Did I have some sign on my forehead that read, "Hopeless Case"? At this point, I wasn't completely immobile, but if the pain and debilitation continued over the next 12 years until I was "eligible" - I knew I couldn't bear that. We left, and again, almost 20 years removed from my lack of answers as a child, I felt like I had no answers and no hope.

Months went by, and I continued to worsen. The pain became unbearable. It got to the point that I'd come home from work and collapse into tears. Thankfully, I was living with my parents at the time because it took everything I had to just work. I remember crying almost every night while Mom would hug me and let me cry it out. I wanted the pain to stop and even said, "I wish Jesus would just take me home." Suicide never crossed my mind, but I was hoping Jesus would just take me so the pain would be over. I was ready to dance in the valley.

A co-worker of mine, Kellie, who shall remain an angel to me forever, gave me the name of her dad's orthopedic surgeon, Dr. Ernie Eggers. She assured me that he was one of the best, and she recommended I see him. What could it hurt? I was simply miserable. I made an appointment.

Dr. Eggers entered the exam room with a commanding yet gentle spirit. He was very tall and not bad looking for an older guy. X-rays were taken yet again, and Dr. Eggers came to the same conclusion as my previous doctor. I needed a hip replacement. It was my left hip, and he would do it. I questioned him since the other surgeon wouldn't do it, and he said, "I've done these on people as young as 17. You don't want to do it that young because it may not last your whole life, but you have to have a quality of life." That was music to my ears.

He also referred me to a rheumatologist, Dr. Gary Crump. He believed the need for a hip replacement at my age could be due to an autoimmune disease that impacts joints. While we scheduled the surgery, we also scheduled an appointment with Dr. Crump. My life was about to change.

Surgery was scheduled for April 27, 1994. I saw Dr. Crump a couple of weeks prior to surgery. I spent almost the entire day at his office going through examinations, blood work, and questioning. By the end of the day, we thought we had come to a conclusion. His first thought was that I had Ankylosing Spondylitis. This is an autoimmune disease that mostly impacts men and affects hips, ankles, spine, and knees. However, the blood test confirming that disease came back negative.

Afterward, the concluding diagnosis was rheumatoid arthritits (RA). But, Dr. Crump made a clarification to the diagnosis—I wasn't a textbook case. I didn't have hot, red flares. My joints weren't swollen and presenting like a normal RA patient. Also, my joint impact wasn't symmetrical— meaning that if I had it in my left hip, my right hip would be equally as damaged. I wasn't surprised. I've never been a textbook case.

After the diagnosis, he prescribed the medicine for treatment and said we'd begin that regimen after my hip replacement surgery. I was a bit in shock over all I had learned in those few weeks, but having answers to my health issues was a new phenomenon that actually felt comforting.

I was more than ready for this hip replacement surgery.

Chapter Eight

April 27, 1994

————— · • ● • · —————

The day had come for my hip surgery. I was nervous but ready to get this party started. When you live with the kind of pain I was experiencing—and I have a high tolerance for pain—you want it to stop no matter what it takes. Even if that means surgery.

As part of the pre-op testing, I was evaluated on muscle strength. Once the surgery took place, I'd have to rely on muscles to help me rehab back to health, so the hospital likes to see what your baseline is presurgery. I found it more than comically ironic that the physical therapist commented on how strong I was. Wasn't it a team of experts from Johns Hopkins that were convinced I suffered from a muscle disease? Praise God, we never pursued that option. Clearly, my muscles weren't the issue.

I don't remember much from pre-surgery that day, but sadly, I do remember waking up from surgery. Or shall I say, no surgery. I woke up from the anesthesia and, in my fog, remembered the recovery people telling me, "We couldn't do the surgery. We couldn't intubate you, and without that, you could have died." What? At the same time, I realized my throat was so raw I couldn't talk. I could only listen. I was devastated. Once again, I had danced in the valley of the shadow of death, and God intervened.

I dressed and went home silent. I had to write my words for my parents, so I wrote out what the recovery team had told me. Needless to say, my parents were livid, especially my dad. We didn't understand. I remember going home and hearing my dad on the phone with Dr. Eggers. The doctor, too, was livid. All we could gather was that I was hard to intubate, so they couldn't do the surgery. My neck had always been stiff (a symptom of the newly-diagnosed RA), and my mouth didn't open very wide, but I had endured previous surgeries with no problem.

On top of the surgery being canceled, my health insurance was changing on May 1. I could no longer go in-network to the hospital I had just left. But that was a blessing from God. Dr. Eggers scheduled me for the next week at Baptist Hospital. To this day, I've yet to see a bill from my insurance company for that first hospital. I have a feeling Dr. Eggers intervened and ensured the hospital ate the costs due to their inability to perform their duties.

Another blessing was that Dr. Eggers signed off for all my pre-op bloodwork, X-rays, and testing to be transferred to Baptist so that I wouldn't have to endure that again for this surgery. I wouldn't realize until later how God protected me by moving me to another hospital and orchestrating it for my good and benefit. This would not be the last surgery I would have at Baptist Hospital, which would later become like a second home to me.

Psalm 46:1 says, "God is our refuge and strength, a helper who is always found in times of trouble." As I sat silently without the ability to even advocate for myself, God was at work behind the scenes to provide a solution that was an answer to the trouble I was facing. No one knows who wrote this Psalm, but scholars speculate that it could be Hezekiah. He was king of Jerusalem when the Assyrians attacked and God delivered His people. King Hezekiah had seen the miraculous hand of the Lord and knew of His power and strength in times of trouble. Later in that Psalm in verse 10, it states, "Stop fighting, and know that I am God," All I could do was stop fighting, be still, and wait on Him. Surgery was rescheduled for May 4, 1994.

Chapter Nine

May 4, 1994

• • ● • •

After a few days, my voice came back, but as much as I was done with the pain, I was a nervous wreck about the next surgery. What if this happened again? My parents and I headed to Baptist Hospital on Wednesday, May 4, for my late-afternoon surgery. I'll never forget my dad wheeling me into the hospital. He kissed my head and said everything was going to be alright. He also told me, "The next time you need a joint replacement, your mom and I likely won't be here with you." Little did I know that 19 years to the day of this surgery, a few years before my next bout of health issues, my dad would leave this world. That would be 13 years after my mom passed, leaving me to face my health journey alone. But, more on that later.

I got prepped for surgery and met the anesthesiologist, Dr. Jue. The nurses all told me he was the best and the one they all requested for their surgeries. As my heart beat 160 beats per minute, he assured me all would be well. He sprayed a numbing substance on my throat, and I soon couldn't feel my throat when I swallowed. This allowed Dr. Jue to be able to perform the intubation. After the surgery, I asked him if he had problems with my intubation, and he replied, "No. Everyone is made differently, and a good anesthesiologist can look at your chest X-ray and determine the best course of action." It was so comforting to have him explain that in a way that didn't make me feel like all this was my fault.

Once I was wheeled into the operating room, the nurses told me a joke—something about Michael Jackson, Tonya Harding, and the Kentucky Derby. They said they'd ask me about it when I woke up from surgery. Sure enough, after what seemed like no time, I woke up and they asked me to re-tell the joke I heard—and I did. The report they gave to my parents in the waiting room was that I was alert and telling jokes.

The first thing I noticed after the surgery was the absence of pain. No pain in my hip and no pain in my throat. I knew the surgery had been a success. I was so grateful. When Dr. Eggers met with my parents after the surgery, he told them, "She can put her name on this arthritis. I've never seen anything like it." That spoke volumes. We already knew I wasn't a textbook case, and even a highly-experienced orthopedic surgeon was surprised at what he saw. It explained so much about why I was hard to diagnose all those years ago. We finally had answers, and I was pain-free. The relief I felt was unfathomable. In many ways, I felt like I had a fresh start on life.

Nowadays, people go home the next day after a hip replacement. Back in the 1990s, the procedure was a bit more complex. I had to stay in the hospital for a few days, and I was on a liquid diet for the first 24-48 hours. Like today, though, my nurses and doctors got me up to do physical therapy very quickly. After about 24 hours, I informed them that I needed solid food if we were keeping the exercises up. And they obliged.

I don't recall taking any pain medication, though I likely had some while in the hospital. My physical therapy in the hospital, though rigorous, was going well, and I went home four days later, on Sunday, May 8, 1994. This was ironically, and appropriately, Mother's Day. It was the best gift I could have given my mom, and Mother's Day became significant in my life again. New life was granted on that day, though in a different way than in 1974.

Over the coming weeks and months, I did the exercises they gave me. I didn't need home health or outpatient rehab. I used a shower seat to take showers and religiously did my exercises twice a day. I progressed from a walker to crutches, then to one crutch. I used that one crutch for quite a while until I felt stable, but I was able to return to work on the first of July. Back in those days, there weren't work-from-home options, so I was more than ready to get back in the game. I felt like a million bucks! The pain was gone, I was mobile, and I began the treatment regimen from Dr. Crump.

This journey to a new hip and discovering my RA was not a road I ever expected to travel. Many people wouldn't look at this and see God in it at all. But I do. Only God could have orchestrated this to diagnose my illness, remove my pain, and restore my life.

You may be in a place where you don't believe God is real or even at work in your life. And even reading my story, you may respond, "If God is so good, why did you have to go through this at all?" You'll hear me repeat this throughout my story: God is always good, and He's always right. How do I know that? Because His road always leads to the best of outcomes, even if it's not the path or outcome I'd choose.

Sure, nobody wants a debilitating chronic illness or to go through major surgery. I had lived my whole life with no answers, yet I still dealt with pain. Finally, I had a diagnosis, a treatment, and surgery that returned me to life with less pain. I was 28 years old and all this began when I was five. That's 23 years I suffered with no hope. But, God knew answers were on the way during those long years.

That simple slip on the ice triggered a series of events that would bring me to a surgeon who was willing to operate. That same surgeon sent me to a specialist who could diagnose the overall problem. Yes, the road was scary, and there was much unknown, but all that happened and showed me God's faithfulness in resolving a chord that had been ringing in my ears for 23 years.

Looking back on this time, when I was given new hope and a new lease on life, I still had no idea how this seemingly mild hip replacement surgery would prepare me for the future — but God knew. You see, when God is faithful (which He always is), we often forget to remember His goodness when we hit the rocky road again. Through my physical health journey, I learned the importance of being thankful and acknowledging how God blessed me—seeking how He was working along every step. When the next rollercoaster through the valley came—which, trust me, there were several more—these practices and mindsets prepared me to face it.

Chapter Ten

2014
Twenty Years Later

———·•◉•·———

T wenty years had passed since my hip replacement surgery, and life
had its ups and downs. My life substantially improved after spending
so much time living with pain that basically restricted everything I did.
Through these two decades, I focused on my career, enduring the uncer-
tainty of acquisitions and closures. I grew in ministry positions and found
a love for mentorship and friendship. My career had grown to managing a
large team and taking on more responsibility in a director-level position.
I was involved in women's ministry at my church and co-leading the ministry as I discipled many, including women facing some very challenging
circumstances. Looking back, those years were my new lease on life, and I
filled life to overflowing, loving everything I did. The mountains overcame
the valleys in life, and though I had a few deep valleys, I kept dancing.

In September 2000, my mom passed away the day after my birthday.
She was a diabetic and had been a below-knee amputee since shortly after
my hip surgery. In early 2000, she was not feeling well—she didn't want
to eat and was retaining water. Her doctor ran tests without any luck.
Finally, in June 2000, a liver biopsy was performed—on the same day my
dad received a pacemaker—and it was determined she had non-alcoholic
cirrhosis of the liver caused by her diabetes.

On my birthday, I spent the entire day with my mom, sitting by her side in her hospital room. She was in a coma, so it was just her, God, and me. I spent a lot of time watching her breathing in and out and also praying. My thoughts went back 35 years to that day when she was in the hospital, about to birth a baby—me. I pondered the anxiety that must have haunted her after all that she'd been through after the birth of my brother. Now she was lying in a hospital bed, living her final days. My heart couldn't grasp what was truly happening, but God's grace comes at the exact moment and in the precise amount we need. I reflected on my life with her up to that moment and thought about all of the future moments she would miss. Death is a cruel thief. I realized that day how much I longed for the day when death would be no more.

My mom passed at almost 6 am on the day after my birthday. Even though she was in a coma, I think she knew what day it was. She lived six more hours so that she wouldn't pass on my actual birthday. Such a blessing from God. Dad was with her when she passed, as it should be. I was 35 and couldn't imagine how I was going to live my life without her. My mom was the bravest, strongest woman I knew. And to this day, she remains the reigning champion in that area.

We had two full days of visitation at the funeral home, and my dad never left the casket as he greeted the visitors. On the day of her funeral, my dad grasped my hand, and we never let go the entire service. It was just my dad and me left, and this time was an indicator of how much we would be there for each other in the days to come.

After Mom's passing, Dad grieved deeply. I couldn't take my mother's place, even though I shared her name. She was the love of my dad's life. They had been married 53 years, and she was the reason he came to know Christ. They never were apart for most of the final eight or nine years of her life. As her health had declined, he took care of her every need. He lived to serve. Now he didn't know what to do.

Eleven months after my mom passed, my dad started dating a widow, named Doris, who used to attend our church. She knew my mom and dad and had suddenly lost her husband five years prior. It was a bit rocky for me at first. Coming up on the one-year anniversary of my mom's death and having Doris in my dad's life was awkward. She was nothing like my mom, but she cared for my dad. He told me they wouldn't marry, but they enjoyed each other's companionship. Doris had never had children, so she had lots of time to devote to spending with my dad.

I was thankful for this friendship my dad had found, but four months later, I truly was even more thankful. My dad suffered a heart attack that required triple bypass surgery. On the day of his surgery, Doris couldn't be there because she was prepping for a colonoscopy the next day.

I waited alone as my dad went through this surgery. Once again, it was just God and me. An absolutely wonderful nurse did the most extraordinary thing for me. When she came out to tell me he was in recovery and I could see him, she warned me what he would look like. Very swollen, with tubes running everywhere. She said he would look dead but that he was fine and it was normal. What an angel of mercy. Knowing I was walking in there alone, she prepared me so well for what I was about to see.

When dad came home, Doris stayed with us to help take care of him—a great blessing which allowed me to go to work. It was good to have extra help—that he would listen to—when he came home to recover. Like most men, he was stubborn, but the two of us could usually talk him into being obedient to the doctor's orders. I could see Dad loved Doris because he would listen to her, even after putting up a fuss. Normally, that was an extreme rarity where bossing him around occurred. It was then that I was even more accepting of Doris, even though she was nothing like my mom.

In February 2002, two months after my dad's surgery, he told me Doris and he were going to be married. Now, I had finally felt comfortable with her, but marriage? Whoa, Nellie! He explained that after his surgery, they both realized how short life was and that they wanted to spend the time they had left together. Shocking as it was, I completely understood. Having my dad happy and healthy was something I wanted desperately. Without Doris in his life, I knew he would have grieved himself to death.

In April 2002, they married. My dad and Doris had two witnesses, and that was it; it was very reminiscent of his marriage to my mom. I was thankful they would have a new life together and prayed they would be around for a long time. Since my mom's death, the fragility of life seemed very real to me. After my dad's heart attack and a triple bypass, I knew he could have easily died, and I seemed to revert to those days when I'd ask my mom when she dropped me off at school, "Will you be back to get me?" Whenever my dad would go to the doctor or complain of health issues, I was fraught with worry. I never showed this emotion to him, or anyone for that matter, but wrestled with the fear in my heart. The thought of losing my dad so close to the loss of my mom was something I couldn't fathom.

Fast forward to Easter 2013, Doris had declined in her health, mainly her mobility. Dad did a lot for her and cooked every meal; again, very reminiscent of my dad and my mom when her health declined. But still, Dad couldn't be happier. Serving someone was what he was made for, and he loved it. On Easter, Doris, trying to help in the kitchen, fell and ended up in the hospital. She had broken some ribs and had other injuries they wanted to monitor.

Easter that year was the end of March, and Dad was faithful to go to the hospital every day, but he would tell me how tired he got walking through the hospital to visit Doris and how he had to stop and rest before heading to her room. That wasn't like him, but I encouraged him to keep taking rests as he needed when he went to see Doris because he needed to take care of himself.

On April 11, 2013, I was at work and got a call from Doris' niece, Christi. I thought it was odd, so I stepped out of my meeting to talk. She told me her husband had taken my dad to the ER with chest pains. Doris was in the hospital, and my dad was at home, apparently not feeling well. He told her he would drive himself to the hospital. Doris was relentless in her concern and care for my dad, even while she in the hospital. She called Christi, who sent her husband, John, to get my dad to the hospital safely. I gathered my things at work and headed there. It was the same hospital where Doris was being treated, and the ER doctor confirmed my dad had a heart attack.

On my way home that night from the hospital, I had a long talk with God. Something inside of me made me feel like my dad's event wouldn't be the last, and I wasn't sure where this road would lead. I prayed a prayer that went something like this, "God, I don't know what is going to happen with Dad. But if this is his time to leave this earth, I need you to help prepare me for that to happen." I will always thank God for the Holy Spirit's nudging to pray that bold of a prayer. In less than a month, my dad would be gone, but God had prepared me to face that journey.

After encouraging my dad to get a heart cath, the findings were inconclusive, other than he had a faulty valve and congestive heart failure. They tried changing medicines, and he was in and out of that hospital three times, trying to determine what was wrong. During one of his stays, Doris was released to go to rehab for her own injuries. They wheeled her up to see my dad before she left, and, oh my goodness, what a beautiful moment. I'll never forget how happy they both were. They reached out to hug and kiss each other, and it was one of those touching moments you see in the movies.

I shared earlier that I was preparing to start my MBA program in July. I had sent in all my documentation and would be taking the GMAT in May. Barring tanking that test, I would be accepted. My dad knew this and was so proud. He never graduated college, and he was so excited that I was getting my master's degree. However, after that April 11th prayer, every time I moved closer to starting my MBA, I questioned that decision. Despite it all, I felt the Holy Spirit telling me to move forward. Pleasing my dad was a huge motivator—nothing made me happier than to making him proud.

Dad was doing okay after the third discharge but then encountered more chest pains at home. He called 911, and I had them take him to a closer hospital—Baptist. He was on a heart floor, where he was monitored regularly. I spent every day at the hospital with him—both during this stay and all of the others before. My dad was astonished at my ability to work remotely. Thanks to technology, I was able to work at my dad's bedside to be there for him and to be there when doctors would come in and discuss his case.

On May 2, 2013, I arrived at the hospital a bit later because I had a doctor's appointment that morning. When I entered Dad's room, he was in the bathroom and his aide was making his bed. He was told to ring when he was ready to come out, as the aide needed to escort him back to bed. Being the stubborn man he was, he didn't ring for help, but burst out of the bathroom and yelled, "Help me, help me!" Then he collapsed.

I hadn't been there very long, and that event scared me to death. I started sobbing as they called code blue. They brought him back to consciousness and asked him his name and birthdate—which he aced. They called in the chaplain for me since I completely fell apart. The doctor came in shortly after and said his heart monitor showed no heart attack or strange occurrence during that time. They chalked it up to a vasovagal episode. But to be safe, they transferred him to the ICU for closer monitoring.

When Dad was in the ICU, he was known as a walkie-talkie, someone who could walk and talk, which isn't common in that unit. They brought him a phone so he could talk to Doris. He was so concerned about her health, and his motivation to get better was so he could take care of her. Despite the collapsing episode, he seemed fine. I had high hopes that he was on his way to going home if things remained stable.

On Friday, May 3, 2013, Dad seemed to be doing pretty well. His doctor came in while he was sleeping and talked to me. He felt like Dad had two issues going on. First, he thought my dad was depressed. Being separated from Doris had caused him anxiety and depression, which didn't help him physically. The doctor wanted a professional to come the following Monday to talk with him. Second, his faulty heart valve needed replacing. At 87, the doctor didn't feel comfortable putting him under anesthesia. But, there were hospitals at Vanderbilt and in Cleveland that were replacing valves via a heart cath. The doctor asked me if he'd be open to traveling for that procedure. I told him likely he wouldn't, but if we told him he'd be able to care for Doris again and feel better, we might be able to persuade him. It would be a hard sell, but worth a shot.

I left that day feeling encouraged that Dad was doing so well. When he was talking to Doris while I was there, he had pulled out his pocket calendar—which was with him always—and was telling her important dates coming up for her to remember. To me, that was an excellent sign.

The next day was May 4, 2013, and Derby Day. Living in Louisville, Kentucky, Derby Day is a big deal. We are the home of the Kentucky Derby, known as the fastest two minutes in sports. Our state is known for our horses, and the entire world looks to our city on Derby Day. Although the rest of the city was celebrating, I was concerned for my dad. When I arrived at the hospital for my daily visit, I could tell my dad wasn't doing well. They had just taken him for a Doppler procedure and discovered a blood clot in his leg. The nurse said it wasn't anything to be concerned about, and they would treat him to dissolve the clot, but watching him go from the chair to the bed was painful. He was weak and needed help. He definitely wasn't the man I saw the day before. My heart sank. I'd never seen my dad this weak before, even when he endured his triple-bypass surgery.

Dinner came and he hardly ate anything. I asked the nurse for orange sherbet. He loved orange sherbet, and at least he ate a few bites. I told the nurse to keep plenty on hand because if he would eat nothing else, he'd at least eat the sherbet. I didn't have a good feeling—I knew a sign of imminent death was to cease eating. That worried me. I gathered some clothes to take home to wash, kissed him, and told him I loved him and would see him tomorrow.

I went home and got the call around 10:30 pm that he coded, and they were doing what they could to revive him. My fears were becoming a reality. I got in my car as quickly as I could, arrived at the hospital around 11:00 and was told he died at 10:54. Both my parents were gone, and I was immediately jolted into the feeling of being orphaned—I was so lonely at that moment.

The nurse called Christi and John to come be with me. They said I could have all the time I wanted with my dad. I sat in a chair in his room while his body lay there, his soul with the Lord, and prayed and thanked God for his life. My dad had told me that after my mom took her final breath, he prayed the same, and I wanted to do the same for him. I sat there in that room, dancing in the valley. Dad had traveled through the valley of the shadow of death to his eternal home, and I had danced in that valley along with him.

My next thought was for Doris—we had to tell her, and she was still in rehab. Christi and John had decided we would all go together in the morning and tell her. I dreaded that so very much. Losing Dad would be so difficult for her to handle. Doris had lost her first husband very suddenly, and now she would hear that her second husband was gone. I'd seen the pain of my dad losing his spouse before, and I couldn't imagine what telling her would be like.

I called my friend Beth. She and her husband, Kelly, came over that night when I got home from the hospital and helped me make calls. They were a blessing and would become my family. Beth has played such a pivotal role in my life, and this would not be the last time she stayed by me in the midst of darkness.

The next morning, John and Christi picked me up, and we headed to the rehab facility to tell Doris the news. She had called me that morning, and I didn't answer. Seeing her number on my caller ID made my stomach drop to my toes. Her voicemail said she tried reaching my dad, but he wouldn't answer. The dread of knowing what was coming almost made me physically sick.

We arrived at the rehab facility, and John instructed the nursing staff to give Doris something to calm her nerves. He explained what had happened, so they complied. John and I sat out in the waiting area while Christi took on the job of telling Doris. I heard the shrieking cries from her room, and I felt the loss all over again.

John and I went in to see her, and she cried and cried, "I was supposed to go first!" I saw, maybe for the first time, her real love for my dad. That picture of losing part of your body, your soul, yourself became very real to me…again.

2014 Twenty Years Later   59

I began to make all of the arrangements for my dad's visitation and funeral, as he had left me full instructions on what to do. My dad was an engineer by trade and one of the most organized people I'd ever known. He loved me so much and didn't want to leave me with all the decision-making at such a difficult time for Doris and me. He always told me he had an envelope with his obituary and details about the funeral and where I could find the envelope. Along with those details was a cassette tape with the two songs he wanted to be played at his funeral. Dad provided the Scripture he wanted, who would do the service, what he was to wear, and his full obituary. His funeral was pre-arranged, so I had all the pieces to the puzzle. My dad was meticulous when it came to details about anything he did. This became even more important when he was caring for someone he loved. When my dad and I moved after my mom passed, he made sure the place we bought would be accessible down the road for both of us as we grew in age. I still live in that home today. He did the same for Doris, allowing her to remain in their home after his passing. He portrayed an unconditional servant love that is unmatched.

When Doris first saw Dad in the casket, I wasn't sure what she'd do or how she'd react. She hadn't seen him since she left the hospital where they both were patients when she headed to rehab. But as God in His perfect peace would have it, she handled it well. She patted his hand, smoothed out his suit, and said how good he looked. What a blessing.

Nine months after Dad passed, Doris left this world on February 10, 2014. She was ready to go see Jesus, and my dad. She'd lost both her husbands suddenly and had lived a long life. Her fight was gone, and she was ready to go.

In July 2015, I finished my MBA with my dad's encouragement motivating me to get through those two years. In the next four years, my work life at QuinStreet got busier, with more responsibilities and more staff to manage, but I loved it. During this time at work, I began creating and leading a summer sales internship program, as I mentioned earlier. I also assumed many responsibilities related to the monthly financial reporting for our division, and due to job role eliminations, I took on more responsibilities. I remained active at my church, teaching Bible studies and co-leading the women's ministry. My love of discipleship continued as I mentored young women. My life was full, and I felt so blessed to be right where I felt I needed to be.

Did I encounter pain? Yes, almost every day. After living with chronic pain from RA for the bulk of my life, I learned to get used to it and press on, keeping my life as busy as possible, living life to the fullest. I also learned to live without my parents, both physically and emotionally. Physically, they were the only people in the world that had been with me through all of the medical challenges I had faced. I rarely shared openly about all I had been through, lest I made myself less "normal" to the world, but I always had my parents to go to when I needed them, the only ones who would understand. Emotionally, I felt lost without my parents. I was only 47 when my dad passed away, and now, before the age of 50, I was an orphan. The lessons they taught me to make a life for myself and be independent would now be tested. I had no other choice but to live on without them here on earth. All was well until the end of 2019. That's when my life took a complete turn—one I never would have expected in a million years.

WHEN LIFE TAKES
A DRASTIC TURN

Chapter Eleven

November 14, 2019

O ver the weekend prior to Monday, November 11, my left knee felt
awful. I could barely walk. I had known my right hip, right knee,
and left knee likely all needed to be replaced after years of enduring pain
that stemmed from my RA. The pain was often low-key intense in my
joints, but most people never knew I suffered at all. I had lived with pain
since I was a young child and had learned to push through it to live a full
life without letting others know what I faced. I also didn't want to let my
physical challenges stop me. The rheumatoid arthritis had been affecting
all of those joints, but now it appeared that my left knee was completely
giving out. After the recent years of caring for my parents and ramping up
my responsibilities in my life and career, my health had gone on the back
burner, but now it was demanding attention.

On November 11, I called the same orthopedic group where my original surgeon, Dr. Eggers, practiced. I knew he had retired, but I needed to

see someone I trusted. They made an appointment with Dr. Yakanti for the next day, and I was thrilled. I needed some relief. I tend to avoid doctors until I'm desperate, so to be thrilled to go to a surgeon had to mean I was miserable with pain.

The next day, I saw Dr. Yakanti's nurse practitioner, Sarah, and she determined from X-rays that I needed a knee replacement. We scheduled surgery for December 10, and I was ready to go. I knew the relief I had with my hip surgery, and that was over twenty years ago; surely, this surgery would lead to the same relief for my knee. Working for QuinStreet, I could work from home and planned to until my surgery because walking was nearly impossible. I got a walker and used it in the meantime, which helped. My appetite seemed to be dwindling, but I chalked that up to being tired from all the exertion to move around. Just a day later, I was watching TV, preparing for bed.

As I sat in my recliner, I couldn't get comfortable. My right hip felt like it had a catch in it. I assumed I had pulled something since I was favoring my left knee. I decided to head to bed and get some rest. During the night, the pain got worse—so intense that I could barely sleep. More than once, I cried out for Jesus to take my life because the pain was too much to bear. I know that sounds dramatic, but I was in severe pain. It felt like continual sharp pains that made my hip feel like it was being pierced with a long sword. At times it would feel like six charley horses that I couldn't make go away, no matter how I turned my leg. My body couldn't lie still because of the pain. When I finally woke up in the morning, I called my orthopedic office to see what I should do. They advised me to head to the ER to get checked out. I called my friend Beth and asked if she could take me. I left a voicemail, and she says to this day, she won't forget the pain in my voice.

Beth grew up at the same church that we still attend today. She's a few years younger than me, but during the early 2000s, we became amazingly close friends. My mom was best friends with her grandmother, so our friendship was meant to be. When I lost my dad and became an "orphan," Beth, her husband, Kelly, and all their children became my family. I love them more than I could ever express.

Getting dressed for the hospital was a challenge, but I did it on my own. Beth arrived to take me to the ER, and I could barely get to her van. We headed to the ER at Baptist Hospital. They took me back and did X-rays and took blood. I had to get an IV, and the male nurse tried three times before he got one to take. Of course, I was already in so much pain, who could feel the multiple needle jabs?

It was determined that I had an infection in my hip. That diagnosis came after they admitted me to the orthopedic floor and more tests were run. The infectious disease doctor, Dr. Klausing, was on my case. Once it was determined I had an infection, they started IV antibiotics and ran tests to see where the source of the infection was located.

I had all sorts of tests run to find the source, but it couldn't be found. They tried to run a TEE (transesophageal echo), but since it was difficult to intubate me, they couldn't get the camera down my throat. They had drawn fluid from my hip—a hip aspiration—and determined the type of infection to make sure they gave me the correct antibiotics.

I felt awful. I remember vividly being so tired. I just wanted to sleep. I kept thinking about how many hours I'd been working recently—both at the office and at night—and how good it felt to just sleep and rest. My life had spiraled into working 50-60 hours per week and pushing my body beyond its limits. Over the past year or so, I had begun having more pain in my right hip than I ever had before, but I kept pushing through the pain. The last few weeks before this happened, I remember how difficult it was to get up in the morning and even get to work. Walking into the office was exhausting. It wasn't the same pain as I had in my left hip before I had it replaced in the 90s, so I figured I had more time before I needed to address the issue. My work continued to consume my life, and I didn't think I could take time to get checked out, much less have surgery. Now the decision was made for me.

In the hospital, I had pain medicine to keep my hip from hurting, and I was finally getting good rest. A physical therapist worked with me to get me to walk, but it was so painful that Beth couldn't bear to watch me. I kept thinking about how good I'd feel once I got a new hip, which is what I needed.

My left knee was put on the back burner due to the issue with my right hip. It all made more sense as to why my left knee had hurt badly enough to send me to the surgeon. I had been compensating for my right hip by putting most of my weight on my left side. As much as that had hurt earlier in the week, it was nothing compared to my right hip now. It was clear that my right hip needed attention, and the left knee would be looked at much later.

Although this all hit me out of the blue in the middle of the night, my disregard for the pain I'd had over the years didn't help. When you have rheumatoid arthritis, you hurt all the time. It's an achy, stiff, sore pain that is constant. It rarely goes away but just subsides. That was my life. When the pain got worse, often it would pass, so I never got too worried. This time around, it didn't pass, and instead got extremely worse. It would take severe pain for me to seek help because chronic pain was my norm. This got my attention, and I was ready for it to go away and get a new hip.

Chapter Twelve

November 19, 2019

• • ● • •

After determining from the hip aspiration that I had an infection, surgery was set to wash out my hip. It was a staph infection, but from all the testing, the doctors couldn't determine exactly what caused it or the source of the infection. I wasn't sure what washing out my hip meant other than the surgeon would clean out the infection in my hip so a hip replacement could occur shortly after that. Dr. Yakanti, my orthopedic surgeon from my appointment just the week before, was assigned to my case. I don't remember much from that surgery since I was fairly drugged up and felt so tired and fatigued from the infection. The surgery went well. Surgery #1 down, and I had no idea how many more were to come.

Much later, I found out from my friends how bad of shape I really was in. I knew I had an infection and felt terrible, but I didn't realize I had turned septic before the washing. Being septic is the body's extreme response to an infection. It can begin to cause your body to shut down. Apparently, that was happening shortly after I was admitted. They told me I looked gray while lying in the bed and couldn't stay awake. I wasn't eating much and don't remember much in those early days in the hospital other than all the tests and being so tired. Beth said she prayed that God wouldn't take me, and when I heard that, I understood how bad I was. Friends staying with me while Beth wasn't there felt the same. Here

I was, dancing in the valley of the shadow of death. Even though I didn't realize how bad my state was at the time, I had a feeling things weren't good. Although I loved sleeping—it's when I felt the best—when I was awake, albeit with my eyes closed, I was thinking; thinking about leaving this world. I felt really lethargic and tired, had no appetite, and wondered if maybe I was going to die. As bad as I felt, it seemed possible I could die, so I spent my time lying in my hospital bed, visualizing what that would look like and what that would mean. I never shared that with anyone because I was too tired to articulate much. I just thought this might be my time to go home to Heaven, and I wanted to be ready.

In 2011, I lost my dear friend Jan who was like a little sister to me. She was originally from Trinidad and had come to Louisville to attend college in the early 2000s. Jan attended my church and was active in serving our youth. We were very similar in our ministry desires and often compared ourselves to Paul and Timothy from the Bible. I never tired of her asking me regularly, in her Trinidadian accent, "What is the Lord teaching you this week?" Jan always kept me on my toes spiritually, even though she looked at me like a big sister.

After she graduated from college, Jan moved to Texas to obtain a degree in radiology. She needed to stay in school in order to keep her visa updated and didn't want to have to return to her homeland. The United States had become her home. Shortly before she left for Texas, she had been diagnosed with lupus. Her small frame—barely 100 pounds soaking wet—was hit hard with the disease. Since I had rheumatoid arthritis, I could commiserate with her pain. In May 2011, I was talking to her on the phone, trying to get her to fly back for a concert in June. Years before, I had taken her to see Harry Connick, Jr., her first American concert, and a few years later, we saw Michael Bublé together. I had recently won tickets from a local radio station for a June Michael Bublé concert in Louisville and knew she had to go with me. I called her back a few days later and left a voicemail to see if she had decided if she would go. I never heard back. Two days later, I got word that she had passed.

Jan had been admitted for a serious infection, and her body couldn't fight it off. Knowing Jan as I did, I was afraid she had given up the fight. I knew she was ready to meet Jesus. In the last conversation we had, she was so downtrodden about having to return to Trinidad because she was almost done with school and had no visa to stay in the States. All Jan ever wanted was to be able to stay here. Now with no visa and having been diagnosed with a chronic illness, I knew she didn't have the fight in her to stay alive. I encouraged her to come for the concert before she headed home to Trinidad. Now she was truly home.

I was devastated. We always joked about having mansions next to each other in Heaven. Now, years later, I lay in a hospital bed thinking about how sick I was and how I longed to see Jan. Granted, my mom and dad were in Heaven as well, but something about this 28-year-old sister of mine being there was such a draw. I felt like I had more life to live, but the vision of being reunited with Jan and my parents was a comfort as I lay in that hospital bed.

The surgeon hoped that the infection would improve in my body and then I could have a hip replacement after the initial surgery. All of this didn't make sense—I didn't understand the washout process and the waiting period before hip replacement surgery. If they could go in and wash out the hip, why couldn't they just put in a hip replacement at the same time? I acknowledged I understood even when I really didn't. I still felt pretty rotten and was getting constant IV antibiotics, so I was sure that we'd be able to schedule the hip replacement surgery after a few days. I didn't realize that my infection was still present in the hip, so replacement surgery wasn't an option.

As the days went by, my temperature was still elevated. I asked if that was normal, and some of the nurses would reply noncommittally. One night, my nurse, Kathy, indicated she was concerned that my temperature was still high, given the washout and all of the antibiotics. She called the surgeon to alert him so that if action needed to be taken, it would be.

On Sunday, November 24, 2019, I met the surgeon that would become my ride-or-die. As I was sitting up in a chair after PT, Dr. Alex Sweet walked in the door. He was 6′5″ and handsome. Maybe I really had died and gone to Heaven!. Dr. Sweet introduced himself and said he was a partner with Dr. Yakanti. He explained that Dr. Yakanti was out of the country, and he would be taking over my care. He didn't mince words— and I would realize just how straightforward he was over the coming months. Dr. Sweet told me that it seemed the IV antibiotics and washout weren't clearing up the infection. He wanted to do surgery to implant an antibiotic spacer. This procedure would use a temporary hip placement that would carry antibiotics in it and work to completely clear out the infection. Dr. Sweet said I would be on IV antibiotics for six weeks; then after two more weeks, my hip replacement could be done.

This didn't sound like great news. Six weeks of IV antibiotics? Eight weeks before a new hip? My head was spinning, and I really didn't know what to ask him. I wanted to get a hip replacement, but that couldn't happen until the infection was cleared. I was trying to process the fact that I wasn't getting a hip for eight weeks. That would be early 2020, not next week. The timeline for my surgery and healing was changing, and I didn't like it. Dr. Sweet was not only handsome but also passionate about his calling. It was clear to me that he wasn't a surgeon that just came in and did a job. He wanted to know and understand his patients. For someone who accepted my case after his colleague left the country, he acted like he had been my surgeon my whole life. His care for me was reminiscent of Dr. Eggers. His words to me were, "You're young. You have a lot of life ahead of you. We're going to get you back to life." I've hung on to those words ever since.

I'll never forget that right after Dr. Sweet left, my friend Christie came up to visit me after church. I shared the news with her. I was still trying to process. After the spacer surgery, I wouldn't be weight bearing, if

I even could get up and walk at all. The thought of eight weeks until my hip replacement seemed like an eternity.

In Psalm 27:14, David wrote, "Wait for the Lord; be strong, and let your heart be courageous. Wait for the Lord." We aren't sure the timing of when he wrote this verse, but it is encouraging as an admonition to follow the Lord's timing. God is never in a hurry. We have our own timetable, but His timetable rarely matches ours. I had to lean into this verse as I faced a seemingly insurmountable task. Dr. Sweet indicated that I might need up to eight months of recovery after I received my hip replacement to return to my daily activities. That seemed like a lifetime, but added to that was the eight weeks of waiting after the hip antibiotic spacer surgery. I just wanted a hip so I could start walking again.

A few days later, my friend Paige came to sit with me in the hospital. She's another member of the super support group that I couldn't live without. Paige is from Alabama, an only child like me, and like a sister. She and I became friends years earlier when I began emailing her while she was serving on a ministry team at the Olympics. A friend had passed along her email, explaining what she was doing, and thought we'd hit it off. We did. We became fast friends and quickly became family. We've shed tears, laughed a ton, and have been there for each other in the good and bad times.

Paige was at her mother-in-law's house in Cincinnati for the week of Thanksgiving and decided to take the short drive to spend the day with me. Later, she shared that she was worried something would happen to me, and she wanted to see me in case it was the last time. Her presence alleviated my nerves as I faced this next surgery to receive my antibiotic spacer.

Chapter Thirteen

November 26, 2019

———·•◦•·———

November 26th was the day of surgery for the antibiotic spacer in my hip. Surgery #2. (You'll want to keep count.) As you walk with me through this journey, I want to let you in on some of the patterns of my surgery experiences. Pre-op is *always* nerve-wracking. You're wheeled into a slot and hooked up to machines that will take your vitals. In this particular instance, I had the same pre-op nurse I had just a week ago. "Weren't you just here?" "Um, yes," I said. I began to share my story, and she remembered me. I would become pretty familiar with most of the pre-op staff in the coming years.

The surgery went well, and I was on my way to recovery. I had been in the hospital for two weeks now and was facing eight long weeks of recovery. It wasn't long after my surgery that the caseworker came to discuss my choice of rehab facilities once I was able to leave the hospital. I would rather go home, but there was no way I could be at home with IV antibiotics administered three times a day and unable to get out of bed. Making a decision on where I would live for eight weeks wasn't something I wanted to take lightly. Could I just stay here so I'd be ready for surgery? That was a no. The rehab that I chose would be my home away from home, so I needed to choose wisely. I was feeling less like death was on the horizon, but having to make that decision was daunting. Lethargy was still present, but psychologically I was in a better place because my infection had subsided.

The staff on the orthopedic floor at Baptist were phenomenal. From the nurses to the aides, I was so well taken care of that the thought of leaving gave me a sick feeling in the pit of my stomach. But it was the next step to recovery, so I knew I needed to focus on that next step. I'd never been in a rehab before, so I had no idea where to start. Researching on the internet is not always very helpful. Few people write raving reviews but rather share negative reviews about how their loved ones were left to die in different facilities. That wasn't comforting.

I finally landed on a decision and on November 30, 2019, I was transported to rehab. It was close to the hospital and where my grandmother had been years before. I remember being so nervous to leave. Due to my spacer and the fact that it had dislocated since surgery, I couldn't imagine any place taking care of me like the staff at Baptist. My nurse that day was Natalie. She was one of my favorites. Who am I kidding? They all were my favorites. I was tearing up as they were packing up my things and getting me on the stretcher. I told her I didn't want to leave. She said some powerful words, "I know it's scary. But God's timing is always perfect. Everything happens for a reason, and this is the next step of your journey." I'll never forget how those words would ring so true in the days to come.

Chapter Fourteen

December 2019

‐‐•◦•‐‐

Nothing says "the holidays" like being bedridden and in rehab. If you can't be a little sarcastic, what fun is there in life? The rehab was very homey, for a nursing home facility. My room had a nice chair for visitors, a huge bathroom (although I couldn't use it), and a large-screen TV, which I didn't watch. Three times a day, I received IV antibiotics, so I got quality time with my nurses. I felt good about my decision of where to spend the next eight weeks. I can think of worse places to be confined to for that long.

I truly was bedridden as we waited for a reclining wheelchair that would allow me to be lifted to sit in a proper position so as not to compromise my hip. This would help to keep me moving and alleviate potential bedsores as I started rehab.

Finally, it came! The nurses and aides would get me on a Hoyer lift, which is a contraption that feels like a hammock but allows you to be transported from bed to chair without getting up. You are connected by four hooks and a swing in the air, moving from the bed to the wheelchair. It was scary the first time, but I got used to it.

The nurses and aides during my rehab were phenomenal. Adam and Jimmy were my two favorite nurses, and since I was on three IV antibiotic doses a day, I got to see my nurses a lot. My three favorite aides were Michele, Tasha, and Sheryl. My goodness, how well they cared for me. Since I was in bed, they had to give me bed baths, which weren't the greatest, but it gave me lots of time to talk to them and get to know them on a personal level. After everything I'd been through, I felt like the world had seen every part of me, so being exposed but cared for like this didn't bother me much.

The food at rehab was actually not too bad. The menu was more diverse than at the hospital, which kept me from getting bored with the options. The desserts were homemade, and even though my sweet tooth had diminished some, I did enjoy the treats. Due to my infection and need to get stronger, I had to drink Ensure every night, a nutrition drink that helps when you cannot get all the nutrients you need from food. Blech. Thankfully, my night aide would bring me some yummy snacks that I could eat with it to keep me from having to drink it straight.

When I reflect back on that time, it seems so unreal. I was only able to do physical therapy in bed, and my main attractions each day were my three meals, snacks, and when I got my antibiotic. The days seemed so long, and because I was so weak, taking naps and sleep came easy. Even though I wasn't getting out of bed during the day, I was advised to take naps. My body needed to recover. I didn't realize how much my body had lost during that initial time of having sepsis.

Being confined to the bed and the reclining wheelchair, I had to find ways to occupy my time. Before this happened, I was a pretty big fan of YouTube and followed a lot of channels. Now that all I could do was watch something on TV or on my phone, I began a new obsession—YouTube cooking channels. Once I recovered, I would be ready to conquer the kitchen! My favorite channel was *Collard Valley Cooks*. Tammy Nichols was the cook, and her husband, Chris, was her cameraman, and they lived in Georgia. I watched her make all sorts of Southern delicacies. Her motto was "Where we cook like Mama did." Biscuits were something I popped out of a can, but she made biscuits from scratch and made it look so easy. I loved her live streams where she would make a whole meal. Another favorite of mine was *The Farming Pastor's Wife*, Leslie Madren. Her husband, Bryant, was a pastor and a chicken farmer. Like Tammy, she would make southern dishes that looked delicious. One of her favorite recipes was called "Cozy Coffee." It's a homemade mix of hot cocoa mix, instant coffee mix, powdered creamer, sugar, and cinnamon, and you just add water. I've not made it yet, but it sounds yummy. I watched them every day, catching up on their old videos and watching a myriad of other cooking channels to pass the time.

My complete lifeline was my smartphone. I had YouTube, Netflix, DIRECTV STREAM, and Disney+, so I could watch anything. I don't think I turned on the TV once while I was in rehab. I was able to have visitors and typically had somebody come every day. I so looked forward to visitors to break up the monotony and to hear about life on the outside.

For Christmas, the ladies of my BFG decorated my room. These ladies were such a blessing. They decorated my room with all the accouterments of the holidays, complete with a pop-up Christmas tree that had lights on a timer.

On Christmas Day, my friend Vana from church brought me a homemade Hot Brown. For those not familiar with the dish, it originated in Louisville at The Brown Hotel and is delectable. The dish is a piece of toast with turkey, bacon, and tomato, covered in a creamy Mornay sauce. Not only was the food delicious, but my time with Vana was delightful. Knowing everyone else had family commitments, I was prepared to be alone on the holiday, but that time with Vana was priceless. She helped organize my room, which was full of gifts and treats people had brought. Christmas looked different, but I felt full in my heart and my belly.

During this time, I had a Pollyanna outlook on life. I always felt like everything would work out eventually. As my infection seemed to wane, I no longer looked death in the eyes. Knowing that this road was leading to a surgery that would return me back to my former life gave me hope. Though the last month and a half had been rough, I knew God was going to shine through. I believed He was faithful and good. When I lay in bed, I began to think about sharing my story when this was over. I even outlined in my head what a written testimony would look like or what I could say if I spoke to a group of women about this time. I just knew God was going to get me through this stronger than ever. I might be confined to a bed, but my will was not broken. That tenacity I had and the faith I held onto made me look to the positive. The time was coming for my new hip, and I couldn't wait.

On December 31, I slept right through ringing in the New Year. When I woke up in 2020, I plopped my Pollyanna hat on and kept my eyes on the prize of a new hip and a new life. This would be my year!

AND SO IT GOES

Chapter Fifteen

January 2020

I'd made it through my first month of rehab, and we were now in a new year. New year, new life, and I couldn't wait. My Christmas decorations were taken down, and I counted down the weeks until I could bust out of rehab and have my hip replacement surgery. Early in January, my social worker informed me that insurance wouldn't pay for all eight weeks of my needed stay. Weeks seven and eight wouldn't be covered because no "care" was being administered. The IV antibiotics ended after week six. For the final two weeks, I was in a holding pattern before I could have my surgery. Without any therapy treatment showing progress, the need to be in rehab wasn't there, according to the insurance company. Not being able to get out of bed wasn't a reason for insurance to cover my stay. I wasn't able to do much physical therapy except for bed exercises, so I couldn't show progress. Once my IV antibiotics stopped, there wasn't a need for daily nursing.

My heart sank, and I didn't know what I would do. Going home wasn't an option. I lived alone and couldn't manage to be bedridden there without

24-hour help available. We discussed private pay and eliminating therapy to help keep the cost low. It wasn't what I was prepared for, but I knew I could pay off the bill over time. My previous Pollyanna outlook began to diminish—maybe 2020 wasn't looking so hot after all. But I knew that, above all, my surgery was coming, and I'd be on my way sooner than later.

I had regular labs taken weekly while at rehab, and Dr. Sweet was somewhat concerned about the results. He wanted to see some of my levels be closer to normal, indicating the infection had cleared. He called me and told me he was about 70% optimistic the infection was gone. Pollyanna here wanted it to be more like 95%. He decided to wait an extra week to give my body time to rid the infection.

When you are a Pollyanna, you always look at the bright side of situations and have a cheery, optimistic outlook. I was certain that given one more week, the infection would be gone, and I would get my hip. I'd been through much tragedy and heartache, and even though I was told insurance wouldn't cover me, I was certain it would get approved. The problem with Pollyannas is they aren't realists. I was operating under the assumption that there was a quota on suffering. I believed that when I had filled my cup with sorrow, it would stop—and I had reached the point of a full cup, or so I thought. I'd been through enough, and surely God would use this as an opportunity to perform a miracle to get insurance to cover the remainder of my stay.

My surgery was scheduled for January 23, and though we couldn't be 100% sure the infection was gone, Dr. Sweet moved forward with the surgery since he had already delayed it a week. My blood work didn't give him complete confidence the infection was gone, but he needed to see the hip visibly to tell if it had cleared up. He was cautiously optimistic that it was gone. I was able to check into the hospital the day before and get back to the orthopedic floor with all of my favorite staff. Natalie was the nurse on duty the day of my surgery. I just knew that was a good sign. Beth and my pastor's wife, Jaylynn, and my friend, Christie, were there.

Christie and I also grew up at church together, and we became like sisters when we both sang in the choir and on the praise team together. I don't know exactly how we became besties, but isn't that the way with some of your best friends? I nicknamed her "my NOK" after my mom died. For my medical visits, I often had to declare a next of kin who didn't live with me. When I lived with my dad, my granny was in a nursing home. I sat perplexed the first time I was asked and immediately declared Christie as my next of kin. She's been known as my NOK ever since.

Jaylynn, and I also became great friends when I began serving alongside her as co-director of the women's ministry. I felt like she was what our church needed as soon as I met her. I was on the pastor search committee and got to know her really well. As we served together, our friendship grew. Pastor's wives can sometimes live lonely lives. They can't share all the intricacies of their lives with just anyone. I see it as a privilege to call her a friend and be a person she can be herself around—both when times are tough and when they are good. I'm so blessed to call her a friend.

I was wheeled into pre-op once again for Surgery #3. Beth and Christie were able to be with me and have prayer with me. My associate pastor, Jeff, was there to pray with me, too. We were all in a great mood, laughing and looking forward to the day we would all celebrate this being over and planning a girls' night at The Melting Pot.

Unlike the previous surgeries, they decided to do a spinal block with Propofol to avoid intubation. I was taken into the operating room, which is always bright and cold, to have the epidural administered. Then I was equipped with an iPhone and earbuds. I could choose the music I wanted to listen to while I drifted off to sleep and during surgery. I chose Kanye West's album, *Jesus is King*. I have no idea why that popped into my head instead of something more soothing, but maybe I wanted lively music so I wouldn't hear what was happening if I regained consciousness.

When I awoke in recovery, I heard the nurses talking about my blood pressure. It sounded dangerously low, as in 70/60. I had a huge warming blanket over me as they tried to get my pressure to rise. I felt weak and thought, "Should I even be conscious with such low blood pressure?" I asked the nurse if the surgery went well and if I got a new hip. Given my history, I like to verify. The nurse said it went fine, but I got another antibiotic spacer—not a new hip. My heart sank. Wait. Someone must be confused. I was getting a hip replacement, not a spacer. That happened in November. But, there was no confusion. I did receive another antibiotic spacer.

Dr. Sweet saw me first. He explained that there was visible evidence of remaining infection when he went in to do the replacement. Normally, they would take a sample and do a pathology report, but he said it wasn't necessary as the infection was still active and visible. They took an X-ray of my hip after this surgery, and the spacer had already dislocated, which meant no major movement for me. An antibiotic spacer is a temporary hip joint that is implanted to distribute antibiotics but isn't cemented or drilled in place. It is meant to be temporary until you receive your hip replacement. Even with a properly placed spacer, you are limited to very little weight-bearing activity. Given it had completely dislocated, I couldn't move much for fear the antibiotics wouldn't move to the areas where they were needed.

I couldn't believe what was happening. As I processed this news, I knew what this meant: another eight weeks of waiting in rehab, and six of those weeks with IV antibiotics. I was crushed, not to mention I felt so weak and my blood pressure still wasn't improving.

After Dr. Sweet left, Beth, Christie, and Jaylynn came to see me. The looks on their faces told the whole story. We weren't laughing and talking about our future plans. I couldn't talk. I had nothing to say. They encouraged me that this was part of God's plan and that His timing was perfect. I wanted to believe their words, but this Christian Pollyanna was losing her positivity. Part of my Pollyanna spirit died at that moment.

I knew what I was facing. I had just been through it and would have to endure it again for eight more weeks. Why was this happening? Hadn't I been through enough in the past two months? I wanted God to explain to me what was happening. This felt like more than I could bear. I wasn't able to see how any of this was good or how I would emotionally and spiritually make it through this all over again. I wanted to go back to work and see my team. I wanted to go back to church and teach my BFG and disciple women. I wanted to go back to my home and sleep in my bed, make something good to eat, and piddle around my house to my heart's content. I wanted to go out to restaurants with my friends and laugh until my sides hurt. I didn't have any laughter in me. I wanted to cry, turn back the clock, and return to the life I knew.

Once they finished their words of encouragement, Jaylynn said, "It's okay for you to cry." I started sobbing. All of the emotions that had been stored up over the past two months came out. Every tear I shed meant a little more of my Pollyanna spirit was leaving me. Where was the good in this? I couldn't see it at that moment. This wasn't the way it was supposed to work out. I was supposed to get a hip so that I could get back to life, not endure another eight weeks of rehab and IV antibiotics. This wasn't the path I was to take.

Isaiah 55:8 says, "For my thoughts are not your thoughts, and your ways are not my ways." My way was a hip replacement that day. But that wasn't God's way of taking me on this journey. This event started me down a path that would make me wonder what God was doing and how I would make it eight more weeks bedridden. I couldn't fathom going through this hard road again. It felt like I was the starring role in a bad rerun.

One part of me wanted to scream: "Why is this happening, God?" and "What am I doing wrong?" and "What am I not understanding that you are continuing to send suffering my way?" The other part of me knew God was faithful, good, and right, and I wanted to be strong through my suffering. But, I didn't feel strong. I felt like I had lost all control, and I wasn't happy about the path I was traveling. I would do anything to turn things around. My pre-op laughter had turned to post-op tears.

Beth told me later that when Dr. Sweet came to the family room to talk to them about how things went, he was devastated. Through this journey, I learned more and more how much he cared for me as my surgeon. You want a surgeon who is passionate about their work and their patients. When I left recovery, I was taken to a telemetry floor to be monitored since my blood pressure was still low. Not only had my surgery not gone as I expected, I was now being taken to a hospital floor that wasn't familiar with orthopedic cases and away from the family of nurses who cared for me so well. I felt like the outcome of this surgery and the blood pressure drop was like a snowball rolling out of control.

Beth stayed with me, but I didn't talk much as I processed the feelings in my head. The thing about Beth is that she knew how I felt and what I was thinking. I always felt safe with her responding for me when I didn't have it in me because she knew me so well. I wasn't happy with this outcome and was in a hospital room away from my normal staff. I felt awful.

Eventually, I improved enough to move to the orthopedic floor and back with my people. After a few days, I would move to the same rehab facility for the next eight weeks. Thankfully, I was going somewhere familiar, but eight weeks sounded like a lifetime. Going through another eight weeks stuck in rehab made me feel numb. I kept thinking about how this road was supposed to be leading me back to my active life, but it was only setting me back further. I needed to wear a brave face, but I was just sad. I wanted a do-over of this surgery.

I was transported back to rehab at the end of January, and I requested to be placed in the same area where I had been before. This would allow me to have the nurses and aides who already knew me. I'd been through a lot, and I needed familiarity. Eight weeks was going to be a long time. Little did I know what was on the horizon. There was a buzz about this new virus that was a mystery to most medical professionals. I didn't understand the concern, and I didn't have the mental bandwidth to deal with any more health challenges than the ones I was facing. Something called coronavirus was starting to hit the news outlets.

Chapter Sixteen

February 2020

settled back into rehab and my former routines. Bed to wheelchair and back to bed. When you are going through a valley, having familiarity is a tremendous help. Learning new caretakers and new surroundings make for a difficult transition. I quickly fell back into my regular routines.

My friend, Karen, made sure I had balloons to decorate my room. A beautiful, large bouquet adorned the corner. Along with Jaylynn, Karen made sure I had plenty of chocolate treats in my "Thank You" bucket. This was a bucket for all the staff to feel appreciated. They knew if they needed a sweet treat, my room was the place to be.

Karen and I have known each other since our preschool days. We grew up at Ninth & O Baptist Church and are the same age. The only wedding bouquets I caught were at her and her sister, Alisa's, weddings. In 2013, Karen went through a divorce. After being married for 25 years and out of the workforce, she felt lost. We rekindled our friendship, and God knew we would need each other—both then and now. When I was so sick in November 2019, Karen would come to sit with me when no one else could. Get you a friend like that.

Even though I constantly played a rerun of the last two months of my life, I was hopeful that rehab was the bridge to my new hip and getting back to normal. I so missed my coworkers and team at my job. At this time, I was Director of Client Strategy and Development at a performance marketing company, QuinStreet. Our division worked with technology vendors trying to reach leads to sell their products. I managed a team of sales support geniuses and a junior sales team that were learning sales and relentless in their efforts. I developed our sales internship program and adored that part of my job. I love nothing better than to take students fresh out of college and train them to succeed in the world.

During my stay at the hospital and rehab, many members of my team and coworkers visited. Even my boss, Mary, who lived in Pennsylvania, came to visit when she was in town. I was so thankful for the people who covered my job for me. My coworker, Travis, came to the hospital after I was out of the woods to get briefed on how to do some of the tasks he was assuming from my load. I believe it took three people to cover for my job responsibilities, but I was so grateful. I was also asked, "Rose, how did you do all this work?" For the first time, I realized my workload was heavy, and maybe it had worn my body down. Personally, I'd rather be busy and active with more plates spinning in the air than is sometimes wise. With my physical limitations, being able to work and serve at my church in multiple capacities somehow helped me feel like I made up for my deficits over the years.

Early in February, when still in rehab, I found out some distressing news. QuinStreet would be selling my division to an acquiring company. I couldn't believe what I was hearing. Although I knew that was always a possibility, the timing seemed to be the worst ever. When you've worked in companies for thirty years like I had, you could see the writing on the wall when an impending acquisition was on the horizon. Even before I got sick, I could sense from some upper-management discussions that our division was being marketed for sale. With this news confirming my worst fears, I now would be out of a job and bedridden, unable to seek employment.

From a Christian Pollyanna, I began to turn into a version of Job from the Bible. First, I was flat on my back and waiting for a surgery to hopefully get me back in action. Second, I was on the brink of losing my job—and my health insurance. I expected the next call to be someone saying my house had burned down. I spent a lot of time praying.

"Lord, what is going to happen to me? I can't live without disability and health insurance. How will that work in this situation?" The questions were endless. I just kept praying, not knowing how God would work this all out. I was grasping the foundation of truth I had built from reading God's Word in the past, since at this time I had no strength to even open my Bible.

Back in 2014, I realized that I didn't crave reading God's Word. At the time, a woman in our BFG talked about how she was so drawn to read the Bible that she couldn't stop once she started. I was convicted that I didn't have that same desire. I enjoyed studying His Word when I was preparing to teach, but to study it for my own spiritual growth? Not so much. I wouldn't always be proactive in studying through Scripture unless I was preparing to teach. In fact, I was hardly ever proactive. I read my Bible to check a box. I did it because I needed to, not because I had a strong desire. I wanted that to change.

I decided to read the Bible in a year. I'd done that before but not for a long time. Surely this would bring about that desire. I chose a plan that included a commentary to help me put context in each passage. I accomplished that task like a good Type A professional and really didn't feel much different. As a Bible scholar in training, I felt like a failure.

Shortly after, I did what I should have done from the start—prayed. Clearly, prayer is the place from which we all should start; however, in most situations, it falls to the bottom of the list. I asked God to give me a desire for His Word. Not just to check off a box or prepare to teach, but a craving to read the Bible. I began to get up earlier each day—which is monumental for this night owl—and spend thirty minutes reading the Bible and praying. This daily commitment to take the time to let His Living Word refresh my soul, quenched my thirst like the 24 ounces of water I drank alongside my opened Bible. It took some time, but eventually, I couldn't wait to wake up and start the day with His Word.

Lest I sound holier-than-thou, the first part of this journey often left me with blank stares. I expected some epiphany or God writing on the wall in my kitchen as I opened up the Bible. But nothing. For me, it was more about developing a habit over time. I realized I didn't need some profound, life-changing moment every day. I needed to be committed to ingesting His Word daily, along with that bottle of water. I wouldn't gain something new every day. But usually every week, I would learn something new or come across something I hadn't read in a while that would stick with me and help me navigate my life. Other times, a verse would ring so true to me that I thought about it all day. When you train to run a marathon, it can take months to be conditioned for the race. This life is a marathon, and to be spiritually girded to experience the mountains and the valleys, you have to train. This was my training. Over time, my desire for God's Word grew, and I was more disciplined and a better student of the Bible.

Looking back on that time in my life, I now realize how God was preparing me. You see, I had a foundation I hadn't had before I started digging into the Word daily. I'd been a Christian since I was eight, but learning to spend daily time with God took my spiritual life to another level and helped equip me to face this road. Although I was distraught when I was faced with losing my job, I clung to the fact that surely God was going to work this out. I didn't know how, which made me sick to my stomach, but my trust in Him grew. And I wouldn't have that kind of trust if I hadn't built a foundation from His Word.

The day the announcement came about our division sale, our Senior VP of Operations, Ashley, called me. Ashley had been the General Manager (GM) of our division for a while, and I worked very closely with her. She was the best, and we became close during our time together. When Ashley called, she delivered the most amazing news. My company would keep me as an employee for however long I needed to keep my disability and health insurance intact. She would be my direct supervisor in the meantime. For employment paperwork purposes, I had to be aligned with someone in the organization as my direct supervisor. Since my division was sold, she became my direct supervisor even though it was clear I didn't have a "job" to return to once I recovered. The CEO of the acquiring company had said he would grant me an interview when I was able to return to work for a potential position.

I was speechless. For all the time I had prayed, worried, and fretted over what my outcome would be, God had it taken care of all along. I thanked Ashley profusely, and she had such encouraging words for me as a stellar employee who had kept this division going through all the GMs we had. I would have no idea how much of a blessing this arrangement would be when this journey became so much longer than I ever expected.

As relief swept over me, I remember closing my eyes and finally resting for the first time in days. The burden of my future had weighed so heavily on me. It seemed there were no limits to what could happen to me, and this job situation seemed insurmountable. I thought again about Job and how maybe I would lose my house. If I had no money coming in and no health coverage, what I had in savings and retirement would soon be depleted from medical bills, and I wouldn't be able to maintain the cost of my house as well. I couldn't stay afloat without disability and health insurance. But God had my back like He always does.

Why do we not trust God when He shows up like that? I know through the journey ahead, and even to this day, I fail to trust Him. Even when He does the unbelievable.

Even with this good news, I dealt with the sadness of an era coming to an end. I had worked with this division since 2011 and with some of these people since 2005 at IT Business Edge. I texted my team and encouraged them, cheering them on. I knew this would be a scary time. I had longed to be there for them. As I dealt with the grief of the loss of my job and my team and the blessing of my personal status with my company, I didn't know what to do with all my feelings. My life had changed and was constantly changing before my eyes, and I just wanted to go back to my normal. When would that ever happen?

Chapter Seventeen

March 2020

---•◦●◦•---

Being at a rehab facility for so long, you are bound to make connections. Or at least, I do. I had many nursing assistants I loved, but one was very special to me—Michele. She would go the extra mile for me and knew before I asked what I needed. Michele gave me many a bed bath, and when you get that up close and personal, you open up pretty quickly.

At this point in my journey, I wanted to be sure I was maximizing any opportunity to share the gospel. I figured God had plopped me right where He wanted me with a mission field at my bedside, so this was my task. Michele talked about faith and about her life and marriage. She had a good husband, and her kids had their challenges, like many families. She also mentioned how they weren't in church. Any opportunity I got, I shared the gospel with her. She would often come into my room just to visit, and I loved those times.

What helped tremendously was the non-stop streaming of visitors from my church. Every staff member visited once a week. My BFG ladies would come and visit each day. Even one of my friends from BFG, Dana, came to do my laundry each week. Michele, as well as the rest of the staff, saw the Body of Christ in action. No doubt that helped as the Holy Spirit was working on her.

On the morning of Sunday, March 8, Michele came into my room and said, "I want to live for God." That started a conversation that led to her praying to receive Christ. When that happened, I immediately thought, "Okay God, *this* is why this happened." There is no illness or even death that is wasted when it causes another soul to follow Christ. I was elated! God was using my bedridden body to share the gospel. I felt renewed and that I could make it on this journey.

My friend, Amber, was in town and was planning to come the next day to do my hair. For a girl who hadn't had her hair touched in five months, I was desperate. I would get my hair cut and colored before my next surgery so that I'd be ready to conquer rehab and get back to life.

Amber was very special to me. She was the first girl I ever mentored. We both grew during that time, as she was growing in Christ with the accountability of a spiritual mentor, and I was learning how to actually disciple someone. She put up with my novice ways and taught me so much about how to share with someone to help them grow spiritually. I sure know that I grew spiritually during that time. I've watched her grow in her faith, marry, and have two girls, and watched how she went from a girl who loathed reading anything to being in the Word daily. Her first-born's middle name is Rose, and I was so humbled when she shared the news of my namesake. Hearing that news before that little girl entered the world thrilled my heart, especially because I previously assumed I wouldn't carry on the name Rose. My mom would have been so excited. After working years as a hairstylist, Amber only does it for a few people now that her day job is working at her girls' school. She has become a wonderful mother; I'm so proud of her. I love her as if she was my own daughter.

The day Michele began to follow Christ, the announcement was made at my rehab that visitation would be cut off starting the next day due to this virus known as COVID-19. I didn't know exactly what COVID was, but I remember one of my night aides asking me in February, "Rose, have you heard about this Coronavirus?" I told her I had heard just a few things but said, "Oh, I'm sure it won't amount to anything here. Seems like it's more prevalent in other countries." Boy, if only that had been true. Now this seemingly innocent virus was causing the world around me to shut down. I'd never experienced a worldwide pandemic…honestly, nobody had. This was the first one we'd seen in 100 years, and I had no idea how this would play out. I was in the midst of my own health crisis and now would have to adapt to whatever a pandemic would bring. I was so disappointed. Not only would Amber not be able to come, nobody would be coming for an unknown period of time. Okay, Satan, I see you, but I know who wins in the end, and I'm on His team.

The impact of this announcement wouldn't completely set in until days later. I had been blessed with daily visitors, even more than one a day, since my recent medical issues started. I began to feel the weight of having no visitors. Any packages or items dropped off had to sit in holding for three days before I could have them to rid them of any possible COVID residue. My friend, Dana, couldn't come to do laundry and have lunch with me anymore. Now the nursing aides would have to find time to do everyone's laundry, making their schedules even tighter and busier. All of the workers seemed frazzled. I would try to engage them in conversation, but they acted very out of sorts, with daily changes to their protocols and responsibilities creating havoc when they came into work. Everyone had an opinion. Some were acting hostile toward management because they had to pick up more shifts for those who were afraid to come to work. The employees with children in school were trying to balance remote learning and their work schedules. Many took the changes in stride, but it took a toll on their emotions. The unknown of a worldwide pandemic made every day stressful.

The whole world was changing, and I felt it, even in my room in rehab. Thankfully my iPhone continued to be so necessary during this time. Phone calls and texts were vital to staying connected with my friends who couldn't come to see me. Connecting with them was important and needed, but I was so down, and they were also struggling in their own ways. Normally, I am the one who would encourage them, but my bucket was empty. Trying to thrive alone and in this environment took all my emotional energy. It was like me and my community were running dry, trying to help one another while taking care of ourselves with nothing to refill our cups.

This pandemic took a toll on everyone. The nursing staff and aides were working in a new environment. Everyone wore masks, and many staff worked extra shifts as people started quitting without notice. Their workload was hard enough, but more work was added and extra shifts given to those who could work, stretching all the employees to their limits. My room became a refuge for the nursing aides. Aside from my chocolate bowl, which was dwindling due to no one from the outside being allowed to visit and refill, the aides would come to me and let out their frustrations. I empathized with them as the rules of their job changed daily. In the beginning, everyone's temperature had to be checked while driving on the campus, and they received armbands to indicate they were clear to enter the building. The wearing of masks was challenging for them in the beginning, like it was for everyone on the outside. As time went on, the nurses passed off duties to the aides because of their changed protocol. It was then that tension began between the nurses and the aides. Clearly, that was evident before COVID. Now with everyone's stress level at an all-time high, adding workload to people already overworked was the tipping point.

One blessing that I received because of COVID-19 was the launch of our livestream church services. For the last four months, I couldn't participate in worship at all with my church family. Now due to COVID, our church would shut down and be forced to live stream our services. What a joy that first week was when I could participate in a worship service again, albeit through my phone screen.

During this time, I realized for the first time that God created us for community. Without the flow of visitors, I had to rely on calls and texts. Genesis 2:18 says, "Then the Lord God said, 'It is not good for the man to be alone. I will make a helper corresponding to him.'" This is the first time in the Bible God said something wasn't good, and He wasn't talking about sin. This was before Eve was created. Although this verse leads to the creation of Eve, a helper and companion for Adam, it is proof that God never intended for us to live in solitude. I had always believed that as an only child, I could exist by myself easily. But I was beginning to realize that no one was created to live as a loner in this world.

I questioned God as to why He would make this journey even rougher by causing me to be restricted from seeing anyone but the rehab staff. My ministry was all around me, but being isolated from my friends and church family seemed like a cruel trick. I just wanted God to answer what His purpose was in all of this. I realized that just a day before, when Michele accepted Christ, I was on top of the world and thankful God was using me in this way. Like an Israelite wandering in the wilderness, I quickly lost that elation when the doors of the rehab facility were locked down like the Red Sea before me. I couldn't wait to have my surgery so I could see someone because living daily in isolation was so difficult.

Everyone I spoke with in the "outside world" was also quarantined and isolated at home, complaining about how hard it was. I was frustrated to hear this because I'd been bedridden for four months. I wanted to be strong and sympathetic, but the circumstances of my life and the world were breaking me down. I felt like I was going through enough without having to be isolated from everyone I held dear. When people would complain about being quarantined at home, I wanted to scream, "People, I've been bedridden for four months; you can do this!!!"

Eventually, window visits would be introduced, where family and friends could visit with us through a window while talking on the phone. Nothing screamed, "I'm in prison," like a window visit. I never had one, but witnessed them and really didn't want to participate.

Before COVID, someone from the dietary team came into our rooms daily to take our orders for the next day's meals. After the pandemic began, dietary wasn't allowed in our rooms, so the food we received was off the regular menu—no changes. If you wanted something different from the menu offering, you needed to tell your aide, who would call the kitchen to order it and wait for it to come to your floor. Honestly, I didn't want to be that kind of bother. I'd rather just eat what I was given instead of causing a hassle. I felt like a prison inmate who was told to fall in line so they'd be treated better.

I began to worry that my surgery wouldn't happen. I had waited all this time, now a pandemic would keep me from getting a hip. Thankfully, my doctor in shining blue scrubs wouldn't let a worldwide pandemic stop him. He called me and said my case was considered urgent. I was lying in a bed with a dislocated hip spacer, after all. I guess there are some good things about being in bad shape. The surgery was scheduled for Saturday, March 21. I would transport to the hospital the day before and be ready for surgery the next morning. He also told me that his dad, affectionately known around the hospital as "Daddy Sweet," would be his medical assistant. With a worldwide pandemic on your hands and operating on a Saturday, you get to set up your own medical team. Dr. Sweet informed me I'd get a "double-sweet" hip. I couldn't wait.

The day came to be transferred to the hospital. I've never been happier to be in an ambulance on my way to see other people in my life. I was allowed one designated visitor, so I knew I would finally get to see Beth. It seemed like years since I had seen her, when it had only been two weeks. Plus, I knew I'd see many of the nurses and aides I had on the ortho floor in the past, and that was comforting. I prayed all would finally be clear so I could have a shiny new hip.

I got to my room and was ready to get this party started. I slept as well as I could that night and prayed that the surgery would be a success. Even though the last surgery I thought for certain I was getting a hip, I did have hesitations at that time, as I knew not all my blood work indicated the infection was gone. This time my numbers looked good, and Dr. Sweet was much more encouraged going into this surgery. Plus, I had his dad, too; that had to be a good sign.

Surgery #4 was a go, and back to pre-op I went. I was nervous but was ready to get on the other side. I'd had hip replacement surgery before and two spacers, so this wasn't unfamiliar to me. All the same pre-op questions were rattled off to me, including, "Do you have dentures?" I always chuckled at that question and wished there was a permanent "No" box they could check so I didn't have to answer that same question repeatedly.

I was wheeled into the operating room and heard country music playing. I suspect this is Dr. Sweet's choice of music to operate by, which made me laugh to myself. They moved me to the small OR table, plopped the oxygen mask on and told me to take deep breaths. I was out. Anesthesia is a crazy thing. You fall asleep but feel like you immediately wake up, which is what it felt like when I woke up in recovery.

The first thing I asked was if I got my hip, and the nurse said—Yes! I was thrilled! Finally, I had my hip and soon would be back to life as I knew it. I couldn't wait to get physical therapy started so I could see how far I could walk. I had no complications in recovery other than my blood pressure was a little low, but nothing concerning. Once I was cleared, I headed back up to my room.

Beth was there waiting, and it was so good to see her face. She assured me everything went as planned and Dr. Sweet was very pleased. I was so happy but still so sleepy from the anesthesia, so I rested as Beth sat there with me. All was well in the world, and I was about to make a comeback. The next morning, Daddy Sweet worked rounds for his son. He told me that he encouraged Alex to sleep in since he didn't have many patients, and he'd take care of them. Daddy Sweet told me everything went well with the surgery but indicated that my right knee was practically immovable, even under anesthesia. He advised me to get that knee replaced within a year. Originally, my left knee was the issue until I found out that my left knee was compromised due to the damage in my right hip. Now, after four months, my right knee was the newest problem.

Although I was thrilled to have a new hip, the news about my knee doused the flame of excitement. More surgery? I mean, I knew my knee wasn't great, and I guess it made sense if it got worse over the four months of being bedridden, but the thought of more surgery seemed unthinkable. I knew I'd need to attend to it and talk to Dr. Sweet eventually.

Right now, I didn't want to think about it, and like Scarlett O'Hara said in *Gone With the Wind*, "I'll think about that tomorrow."

The issue at hand now was physical therapy. My mind was ready to conquer the hospital hallways, but I had no idea how my body would respond. The physical therapists—there were two—came into my hospital room. "Are you ready to stand?" Am I ready to stand? Heck, I'm ready to walk! I assured them I was ready. As I attempted to stand, I felt weak and my legs felt like complete jelly. What was happening? I had gotten a new hip; I should be able to walk now. But being bedridden for four months had depleted my muscle mass to mush. It took a therapist on each side of me, holding me up, to maintain a standing position.

I stood for thirty seconds and was exhausted. We stood one more time, and it felt like twenty minutes instead of thirty seconds. After standing, we finished the session with exercises in bed. I was devastated. I didn't want to do exercises in bed—I'd done those for months. I wanted to walk! I realized my body wasn't ready for that right now. The physical therapists encouraged me on how well I did and said that they'd be back tomorrow.

As I lay in bed, I was frustrated but couldn't muster up the tears to cry. This was going to be a hard journey. I would head back to rehab soon and literally have to learn how to walk all over again...and with a bum knee. For months, I just wanted my life back, and I thought a new hip would give me that life. But, here I was - on the precipice of a continuing hard road that I was growing weary of walking.

I prayed that God would be with me and make me stronger and somehow keep me from getting COVID. I didn't know what I truly needed prayer for, to be honest. I was heading into unknown territory. I had no visitors. I had to wear a mask while doing rehab, which made it hard to breathe. All the medical staff was stressed and on edge, so I found little comfort in commiserating with them. Rehabbing in the midst of a pandemic was a trail never forged by anyone, at least in the last 100 years. But, I was determined to get my life back and willing to drive ahead with all the force I possessed.

Chapter Eighteen

April 2020 - May 2020

———— • ● • ————

A t the end of March, I moved back to rehab. Again, there were familiar faces, but I knew in my heart it wasn't going to be a cakewalk. I would have to learn how to walk all over again amidst a pandemic that kept me away from those I loved, the cheerleaders that would keep me pressing forward.

I wasn't a stranger to the daily routine. And as a routine person, I needed to develop one to fill the time I had without visitors. I couldn't call everyone all the time. Even though most people were hunkered down at home, they had their own lives to contend with. So many stressors came with this pandemic. Everyone scrambled to figure out this new—hopefully temporary—normal, and it wasn't easy.

For me, not much changed except the locked doors of my rehab facility. I was struggling, but I didn't feel like I could lay my burdens on anyone because everyone had their fair share of burdens. I felt so alone. Oh, I knew God was with me, but right then, I wanted people in the flesh. Being isolated for so long had caused me to crave time with others, and they were as trapped as I was.

Occupational and physical therapists started working with me. Unlike my previous stays, I could do therapy without lying in the bed I was ready to break free of. Because I couldn't stand on my own, things started out slowly. I learned to bathe at my bedside until I could eventually wheel into the bathroom. My strength was zapped as my body hadn't done the things it was used to doing in so long. In some ways, my body was unfamiliar to me. I had gone through so much but, until the new hip, I hadn't realized the toll it had taken on my body. Occupational therapists would work with me on muscle building in my arms so my upper body could withstand holding me up. Lifting like a bodybuilder with my two-pound weights, I wondered if I'd ever get strong enough.

Physical therapy started on parallel bars. The only time I'd seen these used was with stroke patients as they regained mobility. I realized these were used before a walker to give the patient more stability. All my therapy was done in a mask, so I felt like I couldn't breathe until I got used to wearing the mask. The first time using the parallel bars, I just stood. Whew. I made it longer than thirty seconds but not much. Each day, we'd work in the bars standing, then taking a step, then taking more steps. I wanted to see progress quicker. I was more than done with all of this rehab. At this point, I had been in the hospital or rehab for five months.

Due to COVID, we only had therapy Monday through Friday. I would work on the exercises that I could do on my own on the weekends and during the day when I wasn't officially in therapy. One of my physical therapists told me to take the weekend off and not do any exercises. You don't hear that from a physical therapist whose practice is also known as physical torture. My muscles needed rest days as they were rebuilding. I was obedient but not happy about it. I felt like more was best when actually it could do more harm. I surely didn't need any more setbacks.

When I wasn't in therapy, which was a good chunk of the day, I had to fill it with something. I tried spending more time in prayer and reading my Bible, but I felt like a broken record in prayer. I would pray for strength and to walk and felt very selfish in my prayers. I worked hard at getting back into the method of prayer that I followed before I got sick. I would start by praising and worshiping God, then confessing my sins, followed by giving Him thanks for the things in my life. Then I would move to pray for others, then end with praying for myself. In the midst of this journey, I had gotten that prayer backward and stuck in reverse. I would start by praying for myself and then never get any further. I would struggle to find the words to praise God. I just didn't have the words, and I wasn't motivated to pray. I had prayed for the last five months, and the more I prayed, the more life spiraled down. I wasn't sure if prayer was even working. I felt like a failure at prayer.

Romans 8:26 says, "In the same way the Spirit also helps us in our weakness, because we do not know what to pray for as we should, but the Spirit himself intercedes for us with inexpressible groanings." This verse is just before that all-star verse everyone quotes when you are in a time of suffering, Romans 8:28; "We know that all things work together for the good of those who love God, who are called according to His purpose." If we've heard it or said it once, we've heard or said it 1,000 times. Verse 26 is what we should say to those in strife. Praying is the most difficult thing to do when you feel hopeless and helpless, so a better encouragement would be to explain that when you can't pray, the Spirit intercedes for us with "inexpressible groanings." Groanings. Speaking for me when I had no words to pray.

Reading Scripture became a struggle as well. When I was home, I had resources, Bible studies, and reading plans. For example, I might read through a book of the Bible, write down the verses, share my thoughts on what I'd read, and read commentaries to help me dive deeper. At my home, I had a plethora of resources on my dining room table, which was where I had my daily time with the Lord. No one could bring all those things to me in this pandemic, nor was I motivated to dive in that deep right now. I was in a fast food-mode. I wanted to go through the drive-thru—get what I needed and move on. My prayer and Bible study attitude mirrored my rehab attitude. "Can we get this train moving faster? I've got a life to get back to!"

Verses would come to mind, but I was slowly sinking without a daily intake of the Word. My body was physically tired, but also mentally. I was spiritually worn down and didn't have that regular "iron sharpens iron" encouragement from my comrades because of the isolation. I could barely pray, much less read the Bible. I was at a point in my life where the prayers of others were sustaining me. There were days when I felt like everything was crashing in on me. I had very little strength. Rehab was so tough. I couldn't have visitors. I wasn't angry at God, but I was definitely angry at the situation I was in, which caused me to have little desire to be in the Word or pray. I knew I still loved the Lord, but I sure did want Him to show His presence a whole lot more than I was seeing.

The rest of my time was filled with my bedridden pastime of watching YouTube videos. My repertoire had expanded from cooking videos to family vlogs. Living vicariously through these families as they recapped their lives in a video made the hours pass. I also began to read again. I read a lot, actually. I found middle-grade fiction very appealing. They were easy reads with less drama than adult fiction. Oh, many of the middle-grade books I read had some drama, but it was much more palatable than more graphic murder mysteries. Thanks to the Libby app, I could check out ebooks from my library to read on the Kindle app on my phone. I knocked out quite a few books during my time in rehab. Reading was another way to pass the time when I couldn't have visitors. A couple of my favorites were *The Remarkable Journey of Coyote Sunrise* by Dan Gemeinhart and *Flora and Ulysses* by Kate DiCamillo. The first book is about a father and his daughter, Coyote, who live in a refurbished 2003 school bus traveling the country. You learn why they are on this journey and the ending is a tear jerker. *Flora and Ulysses* is a story by the author of *Because of Winn-Dixie*, where she brings to life a squirrel, Ulysses, and a girl, Flora, taking us on a journey of superheroes, villains, poetry, and giant donuts. Lots of magical realism that brings the story to life and endears you to a sweet squirrel. Without people to visit, I made books my visitors. I could dive into their stories, and they became my friends.

My physical therapy continued, and I progressed to a walker. I would walk up and down the halls with my wheelchair at my heels so when I tired, I could sit down. I would see other patients zooming down the hallways and tell my therapists how I longed to do that same thing. They assured me I'd get there and that it would just take time. Inevitably, after every therapy session, I would ask, "How did I do today?" I needed the affirmation. If I wasn't hitting the mark, I wanted to know. Going through this time of therapy has confirmed to me I would have been an obsessive athlete had I been physically able to participate in a sport.

A few weeks before I left the rehab facility, my world was rocked. It will likely seem trivial to you, but to me, it was a big deal—and really allowed me to grieve and feel everything that had happened over the past six months. The wing I resided in was being converted to a COVID wing. This wing would be where all new patients came for a two-week quarantine before moving to another part of the facility. I knew this was coming, but I had been in this area of the building for a long time and thought they would at least keep me here until I left. But that wasn't the case.

The administrator and manager came to my room to tell me. I burst into tears. All the emotion I had pent up in me let loose. I pleaded with them to let me stay in the wing I had been in for six weeks—with the nurses and aides I had grown to love. I told them this was the only family I had and that moving me would be devastating. They wouldn't budge and said this was a government rule, blah, blah, blah. I didn't care. I wanted to stay. Nothing I said made any difference.

I continued to sob. It had been a long time since I had cried that hard. The tears were not only due to this news of moving wings but came after six months of hospitals and rehab, multiple surgeries, and isolation from my loved ones. It all came flowing out. I couldn't stop. Surely, the longer I cried, the more apt they would be to let me stay. Or the tears would just numb me from the reality of my life. Thankfully, Michele was on duty that day as my nursing assistant. She came in and held me while I sobbed. When I was able to control my crying, she told me she would box all my things up and it would be okay. Even she was crying.

I had been so strong for six months, and this was the moment that broke me — moving rooms. It felt good to let it out, to raise my voice to the men in charge and plead my case. I was weary, and this was my last straw. I just couldn't do it anymore. I was tired of being strong. I wanted my life back.

It's funny how your resilience can get you through so many hardships, but then one very odd thing can trigger a breakdown. Forcing me to move to a different wing was the catalyst to hitting the actual bottom of the pit. Nothing in my life was what it looked like six months ago, and I was over dealing with one blow after another. I think at that moment, if I had been strong enough to do so, I might have thrown something across the room in hopes it would make me feel better.

Michele packed up all my things and wheeled me to my new room. It looked pretty much the same but was on a different floor. I would have to get to know all the new nurses and nursing aides and share my case with them—and I was exhausted from telling my story. But I had no choice, so I marched forward.

The one upside of my move was I got a new social worker. My former social worker was sorely undertrained, but my new social worker was experienced and compassionate. That was an answer to prayer. She understood my complete dejection of having to move to a new wing and the fears I had of going home. She listened to what I had to say and offered me the facts in an encouraging way, leaving me feeling more cared for than with the other social worker. My last day at rehab was May 12. My social worker had determined how many days insurance would cover, and that was the day. I was so thrilled and so scared all at the same time. As I counted down the days left in rehab, I tried to imagine what life would be like going home. I couldn't fathom living in my house again. Would I be able to function at home? As much as I wanted to leave rehab, I was starting a new phase of life and knew I was still weak. Emotionally and spiritually, I was in a pit. The pandemic had isolated me so much that I felt alone and unable to function with people outside of the medical world. Spiritually I had nothing—my prayer life and Bible reading had become almost nothing in the past few months. I was empty. Putting one foot in front of the other was all I could do, and I was stuck in a mire of not understanding why all this was happening. I didn't know how I would get out of this spiritual pit.

The thought of going home after six months of hospitalization and rehab was overwhelming. Paige had agreed to come up from Alabama and stay with me for a week or so until I was safe to be home alone. Oh how I loved her for doing that! I hadn't been fully alone for six months, but I had been isolated from those closest to me. I looked forward to being back at home and on my way back to life surrounded by my people.

At the time, I didn't realize the day I was leaving rehab to head home was the 46th anniversary of the day I decided to follow Jesus. That connection only occurred to me recently. Despite my excitement to go home, I was still in a pit at that time—salvation was something I didn't think about. I would continue to find myself struggling with my faith as I started my journey to recovery. I had no idea about the spiritual warfare that would follow in the coming months.

As a final check before discharge, the nurse practitioner on staff indicated my hemoglobin was low—7.5. She ordered two pints of blood, which I would receive at Baptist Hospital the day after I went home. Even going home, I had a date with the hospital in my future.

When Beth picked me up, it was such a surreal moment. I was breathing fresh spring air and headed to my house. My home. Somebody pinch me! On our way there, Beth asked what I wanted to eat. I quickly said, "A quarter-pounder meal from McDonald's." Her reply was, "You can have anything you want and you want McDonald's?!" Your bar is set pretty low when you've been eating hospital and rehab food for six months.

Beth and I got home, and as I walked in the door for the first time in six months, I felt like a stranger in my own home. I saw my stack of books on my dining room table-the books I used when I had my devotion time with the Lord each day. I went into my bedroom, and all the sights and smells came flooding back. My recliner was there like an old friend that had missed my presence. I was finally home, and I never wanted to leave again.

Paige, my friend from Alabama, was on her way. My beloved friend and hairdresser, Amber, was in town and came over that day to cut and color my hair. Wow, it was so overdue, and I felt like a new woman! Paige came while Amber was still working on my hair. My people were here, and all was right in the world. I loved being with people after being isolated. It felt like a dream. I was feeling physically weak, but I soaked in this precious time. Being in my home felt surreal, and I was so grateful to finally be home.

For the first time in six months, I was going to sleep in my own bed. Honestly, I didn't know how I would feel in a regular bed again that didn't raise and lower my head or didn't have bed rails. Once I was in bed and the lights were off, I stared at the ceiling. My head was swirling with all the emotions of the past six months exploding inside me. My heart was racing, which was due to my low hemoglobin, so I didn't sleep very well. I knew I had to get up early to go to the hospital for my blood transfusion, so my first night wasn't as glorious as I'd hoped.

I struggled to get moving and ready for the hospital the next day. Paige wheeled me in to drop me off. Getting two pints of blood would take all day. It starts with taking your vitals and your lunch order. Seriously—your lunch order. Because you are there for so many hours, they provide lunch. The process includes getting one pint at a time and making sure you are stable after the first before starting pint two. I was given Tylenol and Benadryl, enabling me to have a glorious nap while in the transfusion recliner.

I awoke long enough to have my turkey sandwich, chips, and applesauce and then slept through the remainder of the transfusion. I knew I was weak and depleted. I hoped that as soon as the blood entered my system, I would perk up like a wilted flower. Aside from finally getting some good rest, the perkiness didn't happen that quickly. When I was done, Paige picked me up and we headed home. The zombie feeling of being weak and in need of this transfusion still lingered. The nurses assured me it would take a few days for that to improve.

Being home was weird. I was so thankful Paige was there since I felt like a stranger in my own house. I didn't feel great, had little energy, and seemed to nap a lot throughout the first few days. Paige was such a great caregiver and cheerleader. She would assure me that I'd been through a lot and my body needed rest to recover, but it was hard to see her perspective. My mode was stuck in "full speed ahead, as fast as possible," even though my body wasn't on the same page. I was just so ready for my old life back I couldn't see what I needed to do to get there.

Part of me believed that going home and being back in my own surroundings would magically make me progress even faster. I'm not sure where my delusional self got that idea other than my drive to return to my idea of normal. I was so glad to escape the confines of rehab, but I really only changed locations—I still had the same road of recovery ahead of me. My body, spirit, and attitude were the same, and I felt pretty hopeless most days.

Paige was great over the next week and a half as she helped set me up for success. We arranged the house so things were easily accessible for me and made sure I had places to sit from my bathroom to bedroom to kitchen if I got weak. Learning to function at home after being gone for so long was overwhelming. But I believe feeling in the pits didn't help my motivation. Emotionally, I was at the bottom of a pit. Looking back, I'm certain I was dealing with depression while processing all that had happened. I wasn't talking about how I felt openly yet because I'd never had these feelings before and didn't understand them. It took all I had physically to get through the day, much less process what was causing depression in my life.

The first weekend I was home, I was slow-moving, still trying to regain strength. Paige was in her room watching her church service, and I was in mine doing the same. I hadn't gotten ready for the day yet and was going to once my service was over. I needed to get my clothes from the closet.

Paige had to me to ler her know, and she'd get out the clothes I needed. Being the stubborn, hard-headed woman I am, I decided I could do that on my own. I have a walk-in closet, and I could easily get what I needed and throw it over my walker. I headed to the closet, and when I reached up to pull a hanger off the rack, I lost my balance and fell backward…into my clothes. I was embarrassed and ashamed. I hollered out for Paige to come.

She ran into my room and found me on the closet floor, sitting on my backside, frozen on what to do next. Paige didn't know either. How was she, by herself, going to get me up off the floor? I knew I couldn't do it myself. What dejection I felt from merely taking a hanger off the rack that caused me to fall. She looked scared, and I stared off into space with no solution. Being on the floor felt like I was physically in the pit I had mentally been in, and the view was about the same. Paige called Beth first, who headed to my house immediately because she was leaving church. Beth, in turn, called our associate pastor, Jeff, and his wife, Renee, for help. Renee is an occupational therapist, and she would know the best way to get me upright. It pays to have friends in the medical field.

I wasn't hurt and didn't feel like anything was broken. I had cushioned my fall with the clothes in my closet, so they became my soft place to land. Beth called and told Paige that Jeff and Renee were on their way. Since I was still in my nightgown, Paige got a pair of shorts so I'd be somewhat presentable when Jeff arrived. That would be my next level of embarrassment if I was not properly dressed with one of my pastors on the way.

When everyone arrived, they began to put their heads together. I felt helpless. I didn't know the best way to do this either and, quite frankly, just sitting on the floor and forgetting it all sounded like a good plan. I wasn't distressed being on the ground as I felt that's where I belonged, mentally and spiritually. I had a shower chair with arms. Renee deduced that if they could get me up in that, I could stand on my own. Now, how would they get me from the floor to the chair? I had lost a lot of weight, but I was so weak I wasn't much help.

Between the four of them, they used sheets on each end of me to lift me up and into the chair. I felt like the lame man whose four friends lifted him down from the roof into the home where Jesus was so he could be healed. But instead of down, I was going up.

The contraption worked! I was lifted up into the chair and able to stand with my walker. I was exhausted. Physically, I was worn out, and emotionally, I was so embarrassed. My stubbornness landed me on the floor. During that next week, Beth came over to help Paige and me conquer my next feat—a shower. I had the aforementioned shower chair for safety but was weak and uneasy on my feet, especially getting in the shower, so the plan was for Paige and Beth to spot me. Trust me when I say that a true friend will be by your side while you are getting in the shower. I did well with no falls. (YAY!) The shower felt glorious! I could count on one hand the number of showers I'd had in the last six months. I had been a birdbath queen, doing all my hygiene at the bathroom sink. I could have stayed in that shower forever, letting the water soak all the way to my bones.

I passed the shower test, and we agreed that after Paige left, I would take a shower and text Beth so she knew when I went in and then text her when I was safely out. It seemed over the top for me, but given my recent dive in the clothes closet, I needed to be obedient.

After I dressed and was back in my recliner, Paige and Beth sat on my bed as we talked. I was exhausted. Have I said that enough? As we started talking, I bared my soul to my two "sisters" because I needed to process what I was feeling.

I shared how I had left rehab in a pit. Not just mentally but spiritually. I didn't pray much. I hadn't read the Bible much. I had clung to what I knew for so long. And I was running dry. During the first few months of this journey, I was the Christian Pollyanna. I knew God was there, and I knew He'd see me through whatever was to come. But after multiple surgeries, being bedridden, essentially losing my job, isolation from COVID, and feeling like a stranger in my own home, I didn't know what I believed.

As I shared all of this with Paige and Beth, they listened intently. I was over all of this nonsense. I wanted my life back—was that too much to ask? I even said I wondered if I was really God's child. What was the purpose of all of this? Why was I still here? Paige interjected, "I never thought I'd see the day that Rose Booth doubted her faith. The one who always was the person encouraging us." I had to agree with her.

I went on to proclaim that if I would have to spend my life using a walker, I'd rather just go home to be with Jesus. Down deep, I knew God loved me. I had that sure foundation. But the termites of trauma had settled in, and my foundation was crumbling.

Beth and Paige were stunned, I'm sure, but they stayed strong. They told me my worth and who I am wasn't determined by whether or not I was using a walker. God had a purpose for me, and He wasn't finished with me yet. I had overcome so much already that I couldn't give up now. I heard what they said but had a hard time truly believing it. After we talked, I was more exhausted. They both prayed over me, and I truly wanted to be back to the "old Rose" again. Life wasn't so bad as a Christian Pollyanna. I wore myself out with my new, dismal attitude, but I couldn't shake it no matter how hard I tried.

This is the key phrase—"no matter how hard I tried." It would take a supernatural refining from the Lord to right my ship. The next few months would be a journey of learning how to give Him the wheel to turn my life around.

Reflecting on that time now, I wish I could have told past Rose what future Rose knew. Being on a walker isn't so bad. Quite frankly, having both legs, no matter how weak, is pretty amazing. I would have told myself not to take this time for granted. I look back at my prideful, selfish attitude and wonder how Jesus still loved me. Though what I had been through hadn't been easy, I really just getting started on that road.

After our conversation, Beth called Jaylynn. Whenever there is a spiritual crisis, Jaylynn is the person you want on the case. Beth shared with her what was going on with me, and she agreed to come over and talk with me the next day. Beth told me Jaylynn was coming to talk with me, so I knew Beth was worried.

Jaylynn came the next day, and she was very matter-of-fact in assuring me that God had never left me and that, for all I'd been through, my reaction wasn't abnormal. When we find ourselves in such traumatic situations, all we can do is simply pray, "Help me, Father". The Holy Spirit intercedes for us when we don't have the words. I listened more than I talked as Jaylynn declared that God had a bigger plan than I realized. She reiterated much of what Paige and Beth had shared, and I knew I would need to look to God to help me out of this pit.

Paige's stay was coming to an end, and I wasn't looking forward to her leaving. I found comfort in her being with me. Jaylynn and Vana had decided to come the day Paige was leaving to clean out my closet. After my fall, they realized my closet was in dire need of cleaning out. I couldn't agree more. All those adulting things had been put on the back burner, in addition to me not being for the last six months.

I'll never forget the moment Paige left. I was sitting at my bathroom counter doing my makeup. Jaylynn and Vana were buzzing around, getting my house in order. Things were being moved around and going as fast as my head was spinning. Paige hugged me, and we both began sobbing. I didn't want her to leave, and she was sad to leave me. As I hugged her, I knew the next chapter of my life was about to begin, and I needed to forge this path with God in the lead.

Chapter Nineteen

June 2020 - July 2020

———— · •●• · ————

When I started living solo after Paige's departure, it was definitely an adjustment. Fatigue was a daily battle, and my body just wanted to rest. I had gotten a new home physical therapist whom I really liked, and that helped encourage me about the progress I was making. My church family and closest friends brought meals, and I loved when people would stay and eat with me. I had been so cloistered away the past six months that I craved interaction. COVID protocol suggested that all visitors stay away or wear a mask when coming to my home. Some visitors did, but I didn't require them to wear one. I wanted to see people and their faces so desperately I was willing to take the risk.

Despite getting back with my people, motivation was missing in my life. Frustration filled every moment, and the lack of energy fueled that frustration. Getting stronger would take time. I knew that, but I had already spent months on this journey, and I was flat tired of waiting. I mourned my life before so deeply. I loved every part of my life before November 2019. I loved my job and managing a team I adored. I loved serving at my church in multiple roles. I loved my independence and having plans with friends on the weekend. I loved going to Starbucks on a Saturday afternoon and reading all day while sipping on an iced coffee. Returning to my old life was all I really wanted. If I had any motivation, it was to get back to that life. That seemed to be my daily mantra. Seven months seemed long enough to endure a trial.

Struggling with my faith, I did my best to be in the Word daily and in prayer. What had become a habit a year ago was now such a battle. I'd never experienced the feeling of oppression until now. I literally felt like I was in a war with the enemy. Being on the brink of denying God and fighting to continue to follow Him was a daily struggle. In my heart, I didn't want to deny Him, but some days were tough spiritually and emotionally. I would fight off the urge to believe the lie that God wasn't there. He didn't care. If He did care, I wouldn't be going through all that I had been through. My emotions were raw, and I wanted to scream some days when I couldn't walk from room to room without being exhausted.

One day, as I was in the kitchen trying to put together my breakfast, I stopped and yelled out loud, "Satan, back off!" The effort it took to make my breakfast—which might be as simple as a toasted bagel and a protein shake—and transporting my food while I ambulated on my walker frustrated me to a point that I believed it had to be a spiritual attack. With every step, I felt I was getting angrier at the state in which I found myself. The pressure to speak against God seemed real—exacerbated by breakfast frustrations. I would proclaim at the top of my lungs that nothing was going to pull me away from following God. It seemed that if I said these things out loud, I might cling more to God. I've never been a person who saw demons behind every bush, but I felt such a pull to walk away and deny God that I was compelled to take action by verbally telling Satan to back off.

On a physical level, I battled as well. Daily tasks would wear me out. Taking a shower and getting dressed were big accomplishments. Making something for breakfast was also a feat. I had purchased a rolling cart that had four shelves. It allowed me to load it up with whatever I was eating for breakfast and move it to the table while walking along with my walker. It was a godsend, but the poor wheels were like grocery cart rejects and, when pushed, didn't always go straight. But the cart got the job done, for which I was grateful.

Due to the issues with my right knee during my hip surgery, the realization of more surgery always hung in the shadows of my thoughts. I had a feeling that knee surgery was in my future. I wrestled with the fact of going through more surgery even before I went to the doctor, but that's often how I process; I prepare myself for the road ahead. Yet, I could never have prepared for this road seven months ago.

The day in July came when I had my visit with Dr. Sweet. He X-rayed my hip, and everything was fine and looked great. Though scared to bring it up, I discussed what his dad had told me about my right knee. Dr. Sweet explained that my knee was really bad and that for my hip to fully recover, it would be best to have my knee replaced. Since I'd played this scenario in my head already, I quickly agreed and said to get the surgery on the books. Had I not already processed that the answer would be surgery, I doubt I would have been so amenable to scheduling it so quickly. I wanted to be able to get back to life, and this was the last piece of the puzzle for that picture to come into view.

Dr. Sweet's assistant, Tiffany, scheduled the surgery for July 21. I was more than ready. After all the time I'd spent in the hospital and rehab, you would think I'd be extremely hesitant to agree to surgery this quickly. But to me, this route was my key to freedom, to regaining the life I'd lost. I was thrilled!

At the end of June, I transitioned to outpatient therapy. I went twice a week and worked with a great physical therapist, Hilbert. He was as unique as his name. Hilbert was an above-knee amputee. He'd lost his leg in friendly fire while serving during Desert Storm and, when he was discharged, had decided to become a physical therapist. Hilbert challenged me a lot for the few weeks I worked with him. He knew knee surgery was on the docket, so he helped me get my body ready. Hilbert had no idea what was ahead for me, but he inspired and motivated me to get strong for the future.

One day after therapy, Vana picked me up, and we headed to Culver's for lunch. As we sat down to eat, I got a call from Tiffany at Dr. Sweet's office. She called to tell me that my insurance had denied my surgery. I was speechless. Are you kidding me? They would begin the process for a peer-to-peer meeting where Dr. Sweet would talk directly to the team at my insurance company to explain why this was necessary. A peer-to-peer approval process allows the attending physician to talk directly with another physician about the denied procedure to obtain approval. Tiffany said she would keep me posted.

I couldn't believe what I heard. Anyone could look at me and see I needed knee replacement. I couldn't bend my knee much at all. After the peer-to-peer occurred, Tiffany called me to let me know it was still denied. In both denials, no reason was given as to why. Unfortunately, this result is typical with insurance companies. Tiffany had moved the surgery out to July 28 to give us time, but now I needed to begin the appeal process.

"Hell hath no fury like a woman scorned," and although I wasn't a jilted lover, my insurance company had jilted me, and I began to use that wrath for my good. First, I opened a case with the Department of Insurance. Did you know that anytime you have an issue with a claim denial, the Department of Insurance for that state can also appeal on your behalf? No? You're welcome.

Second, I asked my insurance company for the specifics on why the claim was denied. They were kind enough to outline them and to also send the PDF document that is used to qualify and approve pre-authorizations for surgeries. I went to the section on orthopedic surgeries and found the areas where I was denied and realized it was mostly based on semantics. For example, Dr. Sweet had documented that my pain was debilitating, but the approval documentation indicated that the pain had to be documented over a three on a 1-10 scale, for a reason unbeknownst to me. Yeah, I think debilitating would rank over a three.

After combing through the document and making notes, I composed a letter for the ages. I applauded them from the opening for their stellar coverage (which was true), and then explained why I felt the denial was in error, outlining each item denied and my counterargument. Color me Matlock, I was in the courtroom pleading my case. At the end of the letter, I pointed out that my pre-op labs and testing were all covered, which indicated that they weren't meticulous in their record keeping to realize that one part of the procedure was covered - the pre-op lab work - while the surgery for that lab work was denied. If they were more thorough, they wouldn't have covered a pre-op claim for the actual operating procedure that wasn't approved. It was a masterpiece, if I must say so myself.

After mailing the letters off, I used my stealth researching tactics to find the email addresses of the CEO of the insurance company in California (where my insurance was based) and the CEO of the overall insurance company. Working in sales taught me how to track down people, and I was pretty impressed with my uncovering of such elite emails. Snail mail could get lost, so I wanted to back it up with emails.

Within two hours of emailing a copy of the letter, I got a call from the California CEO's assistant. She assured me that the CEO would review my email and I would hear something within 48 hours. Hear something? I did. I was approved.

If I could have jumped for joy, I would have, but I remained calm, called Tiffany, and we got the surgery on the books for August 11. I was on my way to getting a knee replacement!

Chapter Twenty

August 2020

————— ·•◉•· —————

Summer was winding down, and I was looking forward to an independent autumn once I received my new knee. I couldn't wait to spend the holidays like a normal person again and not find myself in rehab. My surgery was scheduled for August 11, 2020, after finally getting my insurance to approve. I had prayed so fervently for this approval, and it finally came. Thankfully, I didn't need to redo my pre-op work from July, as it had been less than a month since I had it done. All I had to do was take a COVID test 48 hours before surgery.

I couldn't believe all I had gone through to get this surgery approved but I was glad the day was fast approaching. After everything I'd been through, why did God have me go through this? Was I missing a lesson somewhere? The approval of my surgery began to give me renewed hope in the Lord. I felt less of the desire to turn from him with the hope of my life returning to normal. But as much as I wanted and needed this knee replacement, I was somewhat concerned that maybe I was pushing too hard to get back to the life I had before November 2019. I missed that life and longed for it. But was I pushing for something that wasn't God's will for my life? All along, I thought that my setbacks and delays were the enemy attacking me, but what if it was God's purpose and His timing? No matter which it was, the surgery was approved and a go.

On the night of August 5, 2020, I had warmed up leftovers from a previous night's dinner. My friend Dana, from my BFG, always made enough to feed me multiple nights. I finished dinner and watched some TV, then headed to bed. Around 4:00 am, I awoke with what felt like strong indigestion.

I recounted my evening and what I ate, a Caesar salad with chicken Marsala. Nothing that seemed overly spicy. I got up and went to the dining room to take my blood pressure. It was somewhat elevated, but I was so nervous at this point, I figured nerves were the culprit. Then I decided to take a swig of the two-liter Sierra Mist I had. Don't worry; no one else was drinking it but me. I thought maybe if I could belch, that would solve the problem. Nothing happened. I was fearful of what was happening but tried to remain calm because maybe this was all nerves.

Back to my bedroom I went and decided to try sitting in the recliner and sleeping. It seemed to work, but the pain was still there just an hour or so later. Around 7:00 am, I decided to call Beth. A few years earlier, she went to the ER with chest pains, and it turned out to be GERD. I wanted to see if my symptoms were similar. She said it did sound very similar to her symptoms, but she couldn't remember exactly. I told her I was calling 911 since I wasn't sure what was going on, and she said she'd meet me at the hospital.

Really, God? Now this? I wasn't sure what was happening but I knew it wasn't normal. My dad had heart issues, so I didn't want to play around with potential heart problems. I figured I could just go to the hospital, get checked out, and be on my merry way. I had a date with a hot surgeon in a week that I didn't want to miss.

The ambulance came and immediately the paramedics did an EKG. It showed as abnormal, and my blood pressure was still elevated. As far as they were concerned, I was having a heart attack, so precautions were taken, and they got me on a stretcher to head to the hospital. Once I was in the ambulance, they gave me a nitroglycerin tablet to put under my tongue. I was very familiar with these as my dad always kept them handy.

Riding in an ambulance to the hospital was surreal. I had been transported back and forth from rehab many times in an ambulance since I could only travel via a stretcher. I remember looking outside the ambulance window and seeing neighbors looking on, wondering who was being taken to the hospital.

When I arrived, Beth was waiting for me. She assured me things would be okay. It was so good to see her. Her presence was always a comfort in times like these. Things moved very quickly. An IV was started, and fluids went in along with medications. It became real to me that whatever was happening was serious. I was taken to get a CT scan once the IV was inserted. The ER doctor saw enough and called in the on-call cardiology team to take a look. My blood work didn't show I had a heart attack, but something was amiss.

I couldn't believe this was my *heart*! Of all the tests I'd done for pre-op, nothing showed there was a problem with my heart. Maybe all this was simply very severe indigestion. On top of my questions, the trauma of being back in the ER again was unsettling. Would this be the start of yet another major health setback? I was so afraid this could lead to open-heart surgery, and I couldn't fathom that at this point in my life.

Once the cardiologist, Dr. Chiamandri (we'll call him Dr. C. going forward) read the CT scan, he immediately said I needed a heart cath to determine what was going on. I went into the cath lab, scared yet trusting. How would God allow something so serious when I had surgery in a week to get me back to life? The heart cath was administered, and once it was complete, I was taken to a room on the heart floor to be admitted. Dr. C. came up to review the results and said there was no blockage and he was calling in my GI team to take a look. Surely it was GI-related.

I felt a bit of relief, but my pain was still there. It felt like a big rock in the middle of my chest. If only I could shake it loose, I'd feel better. No amount of repositioning helped in relieving the pain. The nurses contacted the GI team to order a GI cocktail. Now I'm not a drinker, but if this cocktail would take away this pain, bring it on! The cocktail had three medications, which included an antacid and liquid lidocaine. It was supposed to work wonders but didn't touch my pain. I tried negotiating for another one, but no dice. I could only have one of these every few hours.

One of the GI doctors from my practice came to talk to me. His name was Dr. Heine. Yep, a gastroenterologist named Heine. He reviewed my case and all I'd been through and said he would recommend an endoscopy to find out what was going on. It was scheduled for the next day, so I couldn't eat after midnight. That didn't bother me. The thought of eating with this pain was not in my top-five list. I prayed that the endoscopy would reveal the problem. All that was on my mind was ending this pain and getting ready for my knee surgery.

Beth left so I could get some rest, and I decided to watch the Food Network, which is one of the three stations every Baptist Hospital TV has tuned—along with HGTV and the Hallmark Channel. I watched back-to-back episodes of *Guy's Diners, Drive-Ins, and Dives*, the COVID edition. Honestly, it was the last thing I wanted to watch, but I hoped the distraction would help ease the pain.

Guy Fieri didn't help, and the pain kept getting worse, or at least not getting better. My chest felt like I had the worst case of heartburn imaginable, but nothing would give me relief. It didn't feel the heavy pressure everyone tells you to expect with a heart attack, so I had no idea what it could be. I waffled between thinking it was a heart attack or GI-related. I prayed for the latter. It was a discomfort that never let up. As I watched Guy eating food that was delivered to him from one of the *Triple D* destinations, my pain was making me irritable at everything. Am I truly watching Guy eat chicken tamales that were somehow shipped from states away yet still flavorful? I chalked up my hate to the never-ending pain.

Suddenly, nausea hit me so badly that I vomited…all over myself. I don't vomit very often. I can probably count the number of times I have in my lifetime, so I knew something was wrong. I rang for my nurse Brittany, and she came.

The nursing aide helped clean me up, and I could tell Brittany knew I was truly sick. I also knew a symptom of a heart attack was nausea and vomiting. They gave me a bucket for possible future repeats as I calmed down and got back to focusing on the current diner we were visiting via Zoom with Guy, even though I could care less about bangin' shrimp. I wanted to bang on my bed until someone realized how much my chest hurt. It wasn't long after that initial vomiting episode that it happened again. Brittany and the nursing aide came, emptied the bucket, and gave me a cool washcloth. I could see the concern in Brittany's eyes, but she reassured me I would be okay. The chest pain continued. Even throughout these episodes, I got no relief. I was beginning to think this wasn't GI-related.

Throughout the night, as I dozed in and out on the various drive-in episodes, I was only getting minimal rest. This pain felt like it would last as long as the *Triple D* marathon. I have a high pain tolerance, but this was something completely different than what I'd ever experienced before. I'd never had bad indigestion, but I assumed this was what it would feel like. After my limit of GI cocktails, I knew it wasn't GI-related, but there was a rock in there that needed to move. My chest pain wasn't going away, and I hadn't even thought about the endoscopy procedure I was going to have to endure the next day.

When 7:00 am came, so did the nursing shift change. Samantha, the nurse who admitted me, was back on duty. What I learned later was Brittany had called the cardiologist team multiple times in the night to have them intervene. They dismissed it as "not their problem" since they saw no blockage. Brittany conveyed this information to Samantha, and this angel nurse went into action.

Samantha pulled aside another cardiologist, Dr. Rebecca McFarland, and asked if she would take a look at me. Dr. McFarland was the on-call cardiologist from her team, a different team than Dr. C. was on. Dr. McFarland agreed to see me because I had seen another cardiologist in her office a few years prior for a heart murmur. Since I was technically their patient, she was quick to jump in and not worry about stepping on another cardiologist's toes. I felt so relieved that someone else was taking a look at me other than Dr. C. I didn't want this to be an issue with my heart, but after all night with pain, I just wanted answers and relief.

Dr. McFarland reviewed my chart and the heart cath. She immediately saw from the heart cath I had a blockage—a blood clot—in my heart, which was causing me to have a heart attack. She came into my room, introduced herself, and explained that the nurse had asked her to take a look at my chart. Dr. McFarland proceeded to explain what she saw and that she wanted to do an echocardiogram to confirm her findings. She would order one immediately and if it showed what she expected, I'd head back to the cath lab for another heart cath and stent placement.

Everything moved so quickly. I had told Dr. McFarland that I was scheduled for knee replacement a week from now and asked how that would impact my surgery. She told me I would likely have to postpone it for six months since I couldn't come off of my blood thinner until then. My heart sank. All I had fought for and now this. But not only was I disappointed in that delay, I was circling my wagons around the fear of this stent placement and a looming blood clot in my chest.

My dad had a couple of these in his lifetime, and it was a simple procedure. But was anything simple for me? No. I was bedridden and had to endure four surgeries before getting a new hip. Then I was told I needed a knee replacement. Now, I had a heart attack caused by a blood clot. This medical journey seemed so complicated. It felt like those old Family Circus cartoons where Mommy asked Billy to go get something out of the backyard and he took the longest way around the neighborhood to retrieve it. That was my journey. I wanted to be prepared that the stent placement procedure could possibly lead to going into surgery for something more serious. Although that wasn't discussed, it was in the back of my mind. Nothing on this journey had been easy. Why start now?

The echocardiogram technician arrived to do my test. She was sweet and it was painless. I knew I had the right cardiologist when Dr. McFarland came in while it was being done, looked at the screen, and saw what she was expecting. She looked at me and said she was calling her colleague, Dr. Gondi, who would be performing the stent placement procedure. There was no time wasted and before I knew it, I was being transported to the cath lab.

There was comfort in knowing that this wasn't my first rodeo. "Hello, cath lab. Nice to see you again." The medical staff remembered me and began to prepare by giving medicine to relax me. Before Dr. Gondi began the procedure, I told her if I ended up in surgery, to let them know I was hard to intubate. The things you think of in these moments are remarkable. She told me that wouldn't be necessary and began the procedure. I kept my eyes closed and prayed God would allow this to work and I wouldn't be whisked into surgery. The moment she cleared the blood clot, my pain was gone. What a blessing! She asked me how I felt and if I had any pain. I responded that I felt fine and had zero pain. Her job here was done.

Back to my room I went and slept more soundly than I had in the last forty-eight hours. While I was sleeping, Beth arrived. By the time they contacted her to let her know what was happening, I was already in the lab and on my way to my room. For the rest of the day, I was groggy but felt so much better. I couldn't believe what had happened in the past two days, but I was thankful to be alive to talk about it.

Before Samantha finished her shift, I thanked her for being a wonderful, attentive nurse. Had she not alerted a different cardiologist to look at me, I could have been taken into an endoscopy, and who knows what could have happened. She was humble, acknowledging my gratitude, but reminded me it's all part of being a nurse.

Throughout my medical journey, I've come to appreciate nurses more and more. The job they have is hard and often thankless. And when you add a worldwide pandemic on top of that, it can literally be an impossible job. Throughout my time in hospitals and rehabs, nurses were like family when my visitors were limited or nonexistant. They consoled me when I cried and held my hand when I was scared. There are countless nurses and medical staff I may never get to thank personally, but I hope maybe they'll read this book and know how much they are loved by me.

The next day, my ride-or-die surgeon, Dr. Sweet, came to see me. He was somewhat speechless other than to say my insurance company saved my life. Due to the delays, it gave this blood clot time to present itself. Had I been on the operating table with a blood clot in my heart, it could have been life-ending, or at minimum, life-changing. I told him it was more than my insurance company; I knew God was protecting me. We discussed the delay of my knee replacement surgery, which discouraged us both, but I was alive, and that's what mattered.

Later, Dr. McFarland came in to see me. I also thanked her for stepping in to essentially save my life. She said, "God has a purpose for you. He's not done with you yet." Before I even had a chance to drop a gospel seed, boom, she did. That made me even more grateful that God used a cardiologist that I would come to learn was a believer too. God's fingerprints were all over this.

Days before my heart attack, the world tragically lost two pastors I had known. Jeff Fuson, pastor of Phos Community Church, a church plant in an adjacent county where I live and a sister church in my community, and John Powell, pastor of Emmanuel Baptist Church in New Caney, Texas.

Jeff was around my age and had contracted COVID. After a few days, it took his life. It rocked my world, as he had been the lead pastor of this church plant since its inception. The small community where the church was located benefited much from his leadership, and I couldn't understand why God would take him in the midst of a thriving ministry.

John and his wife, Katherine, had attended my church years prior when he was a student at Southern Baptist Theological Seminary. Now, years later, he was also the pastor of a fast-growing church plant near Houston. With four beautiful children, his widow was left to raise them on her own. His death was tragic as he was helping a stranded motorist on the highway. The car was on fire, and John and his friend stopped to help. While assisting the driver, who safely got out of this flaming car, a semi-truck swerved off the road. John pushed his friend out of the way of the semi, and his own life was taken. Again, this story rocked my world.

I remembered this couple and mourned for his wife and four small children. Why would God take this man from the earth and leave behind a beautiful family and a growing ministry?

In the weeks before my heart attack, the deaths of these men haunted me. I took a deep dive online to learn more about them and their lives. I even watched the memorial service for John, as some of his best friends who spoke were former members of my church. The mystery of God's plans, though higher than our plans, kept my head spinning. I couldn't fathom the extreme loss their families felt and the loss their church families experienced. I kept trying to reconcile why God would pluck them out of this world when they were clearly doing so much for the Kingdom of God. Survivor's guilt was plaguing me. Why would God leave me here? I've done nothing but complain about the plight I'm in, but I'm still here on earth. I was beginning to find renewed hope and slowly climb out of the pit I was in, but I still couldn't understand why He took these two men while I remained alive, despite dancing in the valley several times.

The day after my heart cath, Beth came to the hospital to be with me. I'm not sure I could have made this journey without her. I could talk about my deepest feelings and thoughts with her, knowing it was a safe zone. I'd been processing a lot over the past twenty-four hours—the delay of my knee surgery, the fortuitous blessing of an attentive nurse and a loving cardiologist—and dancing in the valley of the shadow of death once again. I felt ready to share more of my thoughts and feelings with someone else.

When I get ready to express all I'm feeling after a time of processing, I typically forewarn Beth. I want her to be ready to listen to all that I've processed so she can help me move forward and make sure she's in a place to hear it. I didn't trust my feelings at the time, so I needed her listening ear to process what was true and what wasn't. I began to share with Beth about Jeff and John and how I didn't understand why God would take these men of faith to Heaven when clearly they had much more work to do. Tears started to flow. I didn't understand why God had spared me—AGAIN—when these two men had such a thriving reach into their communities.

Beth listened to me share and cry. She kept it together, which was unusual for her. We call each other by our last names, and she replied to my outpouring, "Booth, God isn't done with you yet, and He has a purpose for you to still be here on earth. I don't know what it is, but I'm very happy He has kept you here."

I don't know why God kept me here, but I am grateful He did. This whole experience was humbling and reminded me how intricately God is involved in my life. From the nurse to the cardiologist to the delay of my knee surgery, He knew exactly what should happen and, most importantly, when. I was now looking down into the pit from whence I'd come. God had used the events of the last couple of months and the miracles of the past few days to assure me He had been there all the time. Though not back to Pollyanna completely, I had a renewed strength to fight on.

In all the tests and blood work, nothing had shown up as a problem with my heart. I had been fatigued, but that could have been attributed to the months of being bedridden. Dr. McFarland said that my blood clot was an inflammatory clot caused by my rheumatoid arthritis and all I'd been through. Clearly, the sedentary state didn't help, but at least I had answers.

I was released from the hospital the next day and went back home, preparing for cardiac rehab. On August 26, 2020, I went to cardiac rehab and was evaluated by the team to begin my regimen. To say I was nervous was an understatement. I was operating with a stiff right leg and wasn't sure what I'd be able to do regarding rehab. Meeting a whole new staff of medical professionals meant I had to rehash my last nine months of life and see mouths agape at what I had experienced. Along with new medical staff to meet, I would meet other folks in rehab that would ask about my story, and that was daunting. Off I went with cautious optimism and nervous expectations.

The evaluation began with a review of my medical history. Once again, I had to recount the past nine months of my life, which always came with wide eyes and disbelief. My joke was always, "I thought maybe I'd get a baby in nine months, not have a heart attack." Levity seems to be my crutch. Well, my *other* crutch, since I was already using one.

The team tested me on a machine called a NuStep—which I had used in rehab for my hip replacement. I like to refer to this as a seated elliptical because your legs and arms are working at the same time. Can someone fall in love with an exercise machine? If so, I fell in love with this one. It was a way to keep your cardio rate up but not wear out your legs. The anxiety of spending weeks in cardiac rehab diminished slightly, knowing there was a way for me to do this physically.

As I found myself in cardiac rehab, I didn't know what God was doing with this detour in my journey. For the past nine months, I repeatedly expected my journey to come to an end, only for it to continue. What was waiting on the other side? I was anxious to find out, but God had a reason for me traveling this path, even if I couldn't see it.

Trying to put myself in God's shoes is never a good idea. My finite mind can't comprehend His ways. I was minimizing my existence in comparison to these two prominent pastors. God doesn't see things this way. Our view of this world is seen through broken, foggy lenses. Our stories can't be compared to others. I see the past and the present, but I don't see the future. And I don't see the big picture like God does.

Remember John Powell, one of the pastors who passed away and left a wife and four small children? Let's flash forward a year and a half. His wife, Katharine, remarried, which isn't unusual for a young widow. But the man she married, Patrick McGinty, was a special miracle. You see, Patrick worked side-by-side with John when the church he pastored was first planted. They were the only two staff members and best friends. Patrick spoke of how much he admired and learned from John. After a time, Patrick moved on from that position. When Patrick heard about John's tragic death, he mourned greatly. God used other mutual friends in his life to encourage him to pursue Katharine. And the rest is history.

Now Patrick, whose life was infused with wisdom from John, is married to John's widow and raising his children. Only God could orchestrate the other side of that tragedy into a beautiful love story. John's legacy lives on in so many ways.

We're all Johns. We all have the rest of the story waiting to be told. On days when it's hard to comprehend what I've been through, resting in that knowledge brings me comfort.

Chapter Twenty-One

September 2020 - December 2020

⸻ • • ● • • ⸻

The back-to-school season for me came in the form of cardiac rehab three times a week. I'm a creature of routine, and once I had my Monday, Wednesday, Friday schedule in place, I was enjoying the exercise. Even though I arrived on my crutch, I was functional enough to work out on the NuStep. It became my main course of activity for cardiac rehab since my knee was still pretty stiff.

With COVID still a concern and caution, the rehab group at my time slot was limited in number to practice safe social distancing. We were a happy bunch, though! Miss Anne had her heart attack in February and, due to the COVID shutdown, was just now enjoying her cardiac recovery. Frank was a barrel of laughs. He was always joking and poking fun at Miss Anne, who had to be in her mid-to-late 80s. The nurses set the music choices to our favorite channels. Since most of us were in the 50-60 age range, the music of the 1980s seemed to be our jam. I now felt officially old.

My birthday was spent at rehab, followed by a sweet friend bringing homemade Mexican food and a birthday cake to my house to celebrate. I was never one to focus on my birthday, and in a way, a birthday seemed somewhat surreal since I faced death twice in the last year. Birthdays hit differently after you've almost died. Following my heart attack, I was slowly coming out of the pit I was in when the Lord helped me realize

He did have a plan for me, and I was grateful to be alive. Though a quiet day celebrating my birthday, it was another milestone in the life I had been granted. At the same time, my journey wasn't over yet, and my life was still very different than it was before my first surgery. I had a goal to get my knee replaced as I dwelt in the world of "in-between," and I did my rehab and waited. Bigger celebrations felt like something I would experience when I got on the other side of this journey—where I could walk around and be surrounded by people I loved, not in a rehab room.

One of the blessings during this time was getting behind the wheel of my car! I hadn't driven Bluebelle (that's the name of my car) since November 2019. My friend, Jon, who was my resident PT when it came to questions and the help I needed, said he would be happy to help me drive and see how I did. My knee was pretty locked, but driving would be good therapy to strengthen my right leg and hip. I was more than ready to resume *something* that was normal and gave me independence!

He and his family came over, and we got in the car for a spin. Oh, how good it felt to be driving again! To me, driving was a sign of independence. I could freely go where I needed to go and not have to organize rides to go places. My first trip out—which occurred after dark—went beautifully. Jon gave me the thumbs up that I was safe to drive. Jon and his wife, Ashley, were so sweet to later gift me a Starbucks card for my driving achievement. You better believe I drove down the street to celebrate by getting joy in a cup from Starbucks. For the first time in almost a year, I slowly felt like I was on my way to getting back to normal.

Driving was just the beginning of my independent achievements. I went to the grocery store for the first time since my illness. Now, I usually don't go into the store and shop; I utilize grocery pickup. I did that before I got sick and did it that day as well. I picked up my groceries, and when I got home, although it took all I had to get those groceries in the house, I did it! My independent streak continued as I made my first home-cooked meal. I was a pro at making frozen vegetables and warming up frozen cooked chicken, but now I was ready to conquer the crock pot! I made a delicious Italian tortellini and spinach soup. I couldn't believe all that I was doing, but it felt phenomenal.

Once cardiac rehab ended, I joined a local gym. My therapist recommended I join a gym to keep the heart-strengthening going. I decided I would do my best to go three times a week, just like cardiac rehab. I truly believe that if I had a healthy body, even before this illness took me down, I would easily have become a gym rat. I loved working out at the gym! I could have stayed there for hours, but I did put boundaries on myself. There were a few weeks I went four times in a week. I was determined to be strong for my upcoming surgery.

On Christmas, I spent the day with my Blackwell family—Beth and her brood. All day long, I didn't feel the greatest. I was tired, lethargic, and just felt unwell. I went home, and when I woke up the next morning after a good night's rest, I still felt blah. I called Beth and told her I was worried something was wrong, as I didn't feel good. We decided to head to the ER to be safe.

I really needed a punch card to get some services for free after the multiple times I'd arrived at the ER. I was triaged quickly and brought back to a room. I had flashbacks of my first trip to the ER and felt triggered by all that was going on. But given my track record, it was better to be safe than sorry.

Blood was taken, tests were run and…nothing. All my numbers looked fine and no COVID, which is what I thought might be the issue. The ER doctor said I could go home or they could admit me to run further tests to ensure nothing more serious was going on, and I agreed to be admitted. Am I nuts? Did I just agree to be admitted to the hospital? I began to think maybe I needed the psych ward.

Over the next couple of days, I endured a battery of tests. My infectious disease doctor, Dr. Klausing, assured me I had no infection. An MRI showed some stenosis in my spine, but anyone over 40 will normally show stenosis. I was discharged with a clean bill of health, sans all I had been through the last year. But I didn't feel much better.

I decided to see Dr. Sweet. If anyone understood my body, he did. He would know what was wrong. I made an appointment, and when I arrived, I told him how I was feeling and what was discovered—or more appropriately—not discovered during my hospital stay. Being the no-nonsense guy he is, he said, "You've got a horrible knee. You're doing more than you've done in a year. You're won't feel great until we can get that knee replaced." He had a common sense that I obviously was blinded from seeing.

As a 56-year-old woman, I still felt like I was 36. The freedom and independence that I had gained over the past few months had me on the go like someone in their 30s. But, I was in my 50s. I expected to bounce back like I used to, but I couldn't. Not only was I older, but I had also spent months bedridden. Old Wonder Woman here needed to behave more like her age and reflect her current status based on her last year. That was a tough pill to swallow.

The whole world was happy that 2020 was coming to a close, and I might have been the happiest. I lived in a rehab prison due to COVID. I had to learn to walk all over again. I faced death again by enduring a heart attack. I resumed independence in ways I hadn't done in a year. It was the best of times and the worst of times. Around the corner, I could sense a brand new year full of possibilities and knew 2021 would be my year.

THE FINAL COUNTDOWN

Chapter Twenty-Two

February 2021

The blessed day had come! February 3, 2021: the appointment with my cardiologist. I had prayed for this day and that the outcome would be positive. I was prepared to hear that I wasn't released to have knee replacement surgery, but I had prayed that the Lord would grant approval if it was His will.

Don't we pray that often? When really in our hearts, we think, "I sure hope this is your will, Lord, because if it isn't, I'm not going to be a happy camper." I truly wanted His will, but my human sinful side did not want to hear the crushing news that I would have to wait longer. As believers, we long for God to mold our hearts into what He wants us to be, but too often, we're like a preschooler with the Play-Doh. We grab it from Him and say, "Let me help you make that." What an audacious thing to say to the Creator of all things.

Days before Jesus was crucified for our sins, He and some of the disciples headed to the Garden of Gethsemane to pray. Jesus would agonize over what was to come in a garden, like the garden where sin began. In

Luke 22:42, He says, "Father, if You are willing, take this cup away from me—nevertheless, not my will, but Yours, be done." What a moment of complete deity and humanity. In His deity, Jesus knew there was no other way. In His humanity, He begged the Father to take the cup of wrath from His lips. When our prayers don't result in our desires, we have a Savior who has felt anguished in prayer.

I'm sure my heart was racing much faster than it should have been as I waited in the exam room for Dr. McFarland to arrive. She came in, reviewed the EKG and my other vitals, and asked me how I was feeling and doing. I shared with her my successful cardiac rehab and how I had become so independent but hit a wall at the end of 2020, ending up in the hospital not feeling well due to my knee that needed to be replaced. I repeatedly emphasized to her how I was ready to get back to the gym. Beth, who was joining the visit via Facetime, confirmed that if I said that phrase once, I said it 20 times.

After consultation, Dr. McFarland gave the thumbs up for my surgery! I could have hugged her! I was ready for the surgery I had waited months for in order to get back to life. When I left the office, I called Dr. Sweet's assistant, Tiffany, right away and told her I was cleared. It wasn't long before she called me back, and we had a date set for February 16. This would be Surgery #5. My pre-op testing would take place on February 10. That was just a week away!

On the day of my pre-op testing, my sweet friend and neighbor, Janet, was kind enough to drive me. Unfortunately, that day, a terrible ice storm was predicted. Due to the impending storm, the hospital had contacted me to come in earlier to get my testing done to avoid the storm. We headed out just before lunchtime, and on our way there, I got the call from Tiffany that, once again, my surgery had been denied. She assured me that Dr. Sweet would conduct a peer-to-peer and asked me a few questions from our prior battle won to have as ammunition.

The thought crossed my mind whether I should really have this surgery. There had been so many obstacles in my path, all the way down to fighting an ice storm for pre-op. I did pause and said, "Lord, if I'm not supposed to have this surgery, You stop it. You've done it before." I knew I couldn't live forever with a knee that wouldn't bend, so logically, I needed the surgery, but there was a part of me that thought maybe God had another plan.

Janet and I made it to pre-op and back home before the weather hit. I could check this off my list. On Saturday, February 13, my friend, Chad, took me for my pre-op COVID test. This was now a drive-thru procedure, so it was a piece of cake. Chad and I also took a test drive to where I would enter for surgery so I would know how to direct Beth. For all of my prior surgeries, I was already a patient in the hospital, so having surgery like a "normal" person was a new phenomenon.

Although I avoided the ice storm the week before, during the evening of February 15, the night before my knee replacement surgery, a massive snowstorm hit. By the end, we would amass around 10 inches of snow. The hospital called the day before my surgery and told me to be there at 10 am. With the storm, they were delaying the start of surgeries. Now the challenge of getting to the hospital hung over me.

Beth was slated to take me, though she was on the road with her truck-driving husband, Kelly, and it was a race against the clock to see if they'd get back in time for Beth to get me. I was a nervous wreck, more about them driving safely than my upcoming surgery. Janet and her husband, Jerry, were on deck as backup, so I was prepared. Thankfully Beth and Kelly arrived home, and Beth made her way to pick me up. The main roads were fairly passable, but my subdivision was pretty bad. As Beth pulled onto my road, she couldn't get up my driveway. I have a slight incline, and with the snow covering, she had a hard time getting traction. She proceeded to get out of her van, grab a snow shovel in my garage, and dig a path for her to get traction. I stood at my kitchen doorway into the garage and began to sing the praise song "Graves Into Gardens" by Elevation Worship, focusing on this part of the chorus...

You turn graves into gardens
You turn bones into armies
You turn seas into highways
You're the only one who can
You're the only one who can

I sang it over and over as I believed it. God could turn this snowstorm into a smooth highway to the hospital. If anyone could get us to the hospital, it was God. He was the only One who could.

As I repeatedly sang that song to myself, Beth was able to get in my driveway, and off to the hospital we went. At that point, my nerves shifted from the drive to the surgery. It became real that I was on my way to a new knee. I still had doubts it would happen since I'd waited so long for the surgery. And I had that bad feeling that something would go wrong.

I got checked in for surgery and was taken back to pre-op. As I was getting prepped, I looked out the curtain and saw this tall, handsome guy in scrubs headed my way. Dr. Sweet was here, so all was well. He came in to check on me and autograph my right knee, as he does before any surgery, to make sure the correct joint is surgically repaired. As he made his mark, he said, "I have nine patients on the schedule today, and I knew if none of them made it, you would. You would have crawled here to have this surgery." He was right.

Dr. Sweet also told me about the peer-to-peer meeting that Tiffany had told me needed to take place for the surgery to be approved. I knew it had been approved, or I wouldn't be here, but he gave me the details. When Dr. Sweet got on the call with insurance, they recognized his voice. He said, "Yes, you caused my patient a heart attack after the last time we talked." Dr. Sweet told me that after the call, the procedure was approved and the insurance company had actually changed the way they handled these types of cases. If nothing else, all my hassle hopefully helped someone else who would have been denied coverage.

Surgery was successful, and I headed back to the ortho floor and into the care of those who knew me so well. Unlike my hip surgeries in the past, the post-surgical pain in my knee was unbelievable. I had heard knee replacement surgery was much tougher and more complicated than hip replacement surgery, and I could testify. The hip joint is a basic ball-and-socket joint in contrast to the knee joint, which is more complex in providing range of motion and flexibility. Because of this, hip replacement recovery is a piece of cake compared to knee replacement recovery. After my hips were replaced, I had no pain. Even standing and walking weren't painful. The pain of a knee replacement is like having a vice on your knee after it is filled with concrete, and now you have to break loose all that concrete to bend your knee again. Making sure I stayed on my pain medicine regimen was the key to keeping the horrible pain at bay.

When Dr. Sweet came in to check on me the next day, he started by telling me my knee was the worst one he'd ever seen. Okay, he's only been in practice since 2018, so that's not surprising. But then he followed it up with the news that it was the worst knee his scrub nurse had ever seen, and she'd been doing this for 38 years. Now that was more impactful. My patella was fused to my femur. No wonder I couldn't bend my knee. Apparently, with my RA not being treated for months and being bedridden for so long, the bones had fused together. We'll never know for sure, but that was our assumption. He told me that it went very well, but physical therapy needed to be easy as all the soft tissue around the replacement needed to heal as well. Due to that, I could only bear partial weight at first.

Physical therapy started immediately, and I was determined to excel, despite the pain. I had a choice of going home or returning to my previous rehab facility. I was nervous to go home since I was partial weight-bearing, so I decided to go to rehab. Reflecting on that decision now, I still believe it was the right one. My body was weak from all it had been through, and I was nervous about not having constant care. But, part of me dreaded heading back to rehab prison.

After a short stay at the hospital, I returned to the dreaded rehab. Due to COVID, I was transported from the hospital alone and feeling pretty discouraged. My pain wasn't subsiding, and I loathed the thought of being there again. The last time was so very traumatizing. Here I was for the third time, sitting in the lobby with my belongings, waiting for someone to take me to my room. Please let it be someone nice.

An aide came to retrieve me and take me to my room. I tried to make small talk and get to know her. Even through my pain, I wanted to make a friend. I got settled enough until a nurse could get more pain meds. The worst part was I had no walker until the next day when the physical therapist would assess me.

After I got settled in, it wasn't long until shift change. The new aide I had was not very friendly…even when I tried to get to know her and make small talk. She looked like she hated life and her job. This was common in the midst of COVID when employees were worn down from working too many hours. Nothing I said would get her to open up and talk more. When I called for her to help me get into bed for the night, she came. I got dressed for bed, and when I was getting into bed, I broke down sobbing, releasing all of the emotions from being back in rehab. At that point, her attitude changed. She asked me what was wrong, and I told her I didn't want to be there and explained my last two years of life. From then on, she was different towards me, and though I hated breaking down with her, I'm thankful it caused her to treat me differently. She opened up more over time and became my favorite night aide.

The days to come were filled with physical and occupational therapy. I did well even though my knee was killing me. That was to be expected. I was walking longer around the rehab gym and was able to do the NuStep machine. Although I had so much pain, my therapists assured me it was normal and I was progressing well. This positive news was the glimmer of hope I'd been waiting for. It wouldn't be long before I would progress home!

Chapter Twenty-Three

March 2021

⸱•●•⸱

The new month made me excited that I would be going home soon! I was improving in rehab, and although I didn't feel like a master at anything, I did feel like I could get there. It seemed almost too good to be true, but I really felt like the end of this journey was near.

On March 3, I accomplished the huge task of getting ready without assistance from my occupational therapist. I was able to walk to and from the bathroom and get dressed without many issues at all. I achieved the goal that I knew would be the ticket for me to go home, even though the pain was still there.

Later that day, my physical therapist took me to the gym. I knew we'd do the NuStep machine to get warmed up, then walk. After the NuStep, we worked on some stretching and headed toward walking. My PT started wheeling me across the gym without using the leg rests on my wheelchair, and my right leg, the one with the newly-replaced knee, bent under the wheelchair as he pushed me forward.

I heard a lot of crunching as my knee bent backward further than it ever had in my lifetime. The pain was unbelievable. Tears came streaming out of my eyes due to the pain. I couldn't believe what I was feeling and what had just happened. If I thought the pain from the surgery was bad, this was so much worse. The thoughts ran through my head that something horrible had happened while my therapist assured me what I heard was just scar tissue breaking up.

As I was rolled back to my room, dejected and devastated, I couldn't even think straight due to the pain. I knew I had to see Dr. Sweet. In fact, I wanted to call him right then. I knew he would take care of me. I felt like no one at rehab thought it was serious. I wanted to cry, but really all I wanted to do was sleep to make the pain go away.

Soon after my injury, the PT manager came and, like my therapist, thought this was merely scar tissue that was breaking up. I didn't agree. All I knew was Dr. Sweet had been very specific in my orders to be gentle with my knee while in therapy so it could heal well. Even the nurse practitioner in charge of my medical care didn't seem concerned. If I hadn't been in so much pain, I would have fought back harder for them to check me out further with an X-ray or something more extensive, but it hurt too much for me to think. My physical therapy even continued over the next few days, with me using the NuStep through the most excruciating pain I'd ever had. No one at rehab thought there was any problem.

It was time to take my health into my own hands. I called Dr. Sweet's office, talked to his medical assistant, Tiffany, and explained what happened. She talked to Dr. Sweet, and he wanted me to come in right away. The staff at rehab seemed a bit surprised I had made an appointment, which further concerned me. Something was wrong, and I needed my ride-or-die to check me out.

Arriving at Dr. Sweet's office was bittersweet. I longed to see him so he could solve my issue, but I was scared of the outcome. As I explained what happened, he had me do a few things with my right leg. Then he put his head in his hands. Under his breath, I heard him say, "I told them to be cautious with your leg."

He told me he suspected my patella tendon had torn. He confirmed the diagnosis with an X-ray. I knew the answer here would be more surgery, and it was. Dr. Sweet wanted to talk with his colleagues about options for repair before committing to what he would do. He said he would call me tomorrow with an answer.

I left his office numb and defeated. I was so close to going home, but now it seemed more surgery, rehab, and healing were on the horizon. Where was God in all of this? Had I not suffered enough already? I knew God was there, but I was trying with all my might to make sense of what was happening. I just wanted to get back to life and serve Him. Why was this journey taking *so* long with *so* many detours? I was so close to going home and starting outpatient rehab and returning to my life that I could smell it and even touch it. In the crushing of my tendon, my life had gone backward in an instant, and I couldn't grasp in my head what all of this would mean. I had traveled out of the pit and was focusing ahead on returning to my life, and now I endured another setback. The fear of slipping into that pit again came rushing toward me as I considered what the next few months might look like.

I would often replay the traumatic incident in my mind. How it happened. How it felt. How it sounded. The sound of the tearing of my tendon was like a pot full of popcorn emerging from the hot oil. The pain rivaled what I felt in November 2019 when this journey started. Part of me wished I had kept my stiff knee and avoided the pain from the replacement surgery and the tendon repair altogether.

Returning to rehab with this diagnosis of a torn patella tendon brought surprise to the rehab team. I was frustrated that medical professionals had considered this non-urgent, ignoring my pleas that something was wrong. I was angry, thinking that I wouldn't have gotten the medical attention I needed if I wasn't my own advocate. Thankfully, after having that diagnosis and new orders from Dr. Sweet, they did not put me through the rigor of physical therapy. I was simply there to wait to return to the hospital for surgery.

Dr. Sweet called me the day after my appointment and said he had discussed it with his dad, who had agreed to be in surgery to use a technique to repair the tendon. The Sweet Dynamic Duo would once again work together to fix my issue. Confidence grew in me that this surgery would go well, and then I could continue getting back to life. Exiting the doors of rehab felt so good, even though I was headed to impending surgery.

On March 16, one month to the day after my knee replacement, I had the surgery to repair my patella tendon. This was Surgery #6. I was told that I was partial weight-bearing and that the surgery went well. We'd now have to give the tendon about four to six weeks to heal, and then I could return to rehab for my knee.

As you can imagine, I did not want to go back to the same rehab. I wanted to go home while my knee healed. Insurance would only cover a rehab stay if you were actually doing rehab. I wouldn't be able to do rehab for four to six weeks, so I knew going to rehab was pointless. Plus, the idea of stepping back in the facility where all this happened was very traumatic. Being trapped there for four months in 2019 was hard enough, then a pandemic hit, keeping me even more confined. When I returned, I spent two more months learning to walk all over again while breathing through a mask and cut off from my friends. The third time I went, I arrived alone, breaking down at the thought of going through this again while being imprisoned. Then my patella tendon tore within days of my discharge due to a lack of care. Merely rolling through the front door would bring back a flood of those memories.

Beth came to the hospital and encouraged me to go to rehab to heal. She (as did many other friends who had talked with her) felt that I wasn't strong or stable enough to go home for the four to six weeks of healing time. I agreed, though with a bit of disdain, knowing that insurance wouldn't pay for my stay. Beth and other friends, who were my key caregivers during this time, all agreed going to rehab was best. I couldn't argue with them, so I agreed to go and see what happened. I knew I wouldn't be approved to be in rehab for long and figured I could deal with a shorter stay.

The day came for discharge, and here I was, returning to the scene of the accident. I was nervous and scared, but I knew I had to go through the motions, even though I was pretty confident I'd be home soon, depending on how long insurance would allow me to stay in rehab. I arrived late in the day and couldn't get a walker again that first day. Getting to the bed was a disaster. The aide had to help me, and I almost fell. I just wanted all of this to be over. The next day, I met with the nurse practitioner, the PT manager, the OT manager, and my caseworker. Insurance wanted an update within 24 hours, so they were pretty certain they wouldn't be paying. I knew this was the case, as I had become certified in decoding insurance coverage this past year and a half.

Along with this discussion, they had the boldness to tell me that part of my last stay had not been covered. They didn't say why, but it was likely due to not being able to do physical therapy during the last week of my stay, given my torn patella tendon. I quickly bristled and let them know that I was here longer due to their negligence in my care. That topic quickly got squelched.

Within 24 hours, I was being packed up to head home. I expected this outcome since I knew how insurance coverage works when you can't do any therapy. My friends were adamant that I go to rehab, and we tried, but I was going home. Paige would come to stay with me for a week, and I was ready to get past this initial holding pattern and start rehab on my knee. Life at home was somewhat difficult since I was partial weight-bearing. I had an immobilizer on my leg, which helped to keep it straight. Again, I was learning how to do life in a new way.

Unlike when I left rehab in May 2020, I wasn't completely in a pit emotionally and spiritually. The Lord had truly restored my hope that I would improve. This setback had put me on the precipice of falling quickly back into the pit, so I hung onto the edge, grasping it tenaciously so as not to fall. When I felt as though I was beginning to slide toward that pit, I began to look at this as just a small blip in the journey. Getting my tendon stronger would help support my new knee, and that was encouraging. It was now March, and I knew spring was on its way—warmer weather, more sunshine—I was clinging to hope. Losing my mobility to this level wasn't encouraging, but March sadness would surely bring April gladness.

Chapter Twenty-Four

April 2021 - May 2021

· • ● • ·

With the freshness of warmer weather in the air and many pandemic restrictions lifting, I was enjoying the freedom of being in my own home, even if that meant most of my day was spent in a recliner. I've always had a recliner in my bedroom, and it has been one of my favorite places to watch television or read. Now it was my permanent spot for everything. I was waiting for my leg to heal, but even more importantly, I was waiting for my incision to heal.

As I changed my dressing daily, the incision just didn't seem to be closing up. Due to my RA, I knew my healing would be very slow, but this seemed more than just healing taking its time. I was due to see Dr. Sweet soon, and I knew he would know what to do. He had been seeing me every two weeks to keep up with the progress of healing, and since my last visit with him on March 29, I wasn't sure things were headed in the right direction. We noticed my incision wasn't closing that day, and since then, I had been closely monitoring it during my daily dressing change.

I went to see him on April 12. It's a day I will never forget. When he removed the dressing, he had that same defeated look the day I saw him for my patella tendon tear. He was upset and rattled. He wanted to take a wound culture, and I asked him, "Dr. Sweet, am I going to be okay?" His response was, "I don't know." He looked like he was going to lose it; then he walked out of the room to get the wound culture kit.

I fell apart and started crying. As goes Dr. Sweet, so go I. If he's down, I'm down. If he's upbeat, I'm upbeat. Beth was with me, and she had to keep me calm. I didn't know what any of this meant. Was my incision infected? What was going to happen? Did this mean more surgery? My head was spinning.

After a while, Dr. Sweet came back into the room. He was composed and gave me a pep talk. He told me that he thought my incision was infected and wanted to do a washout to clean it up, remove any infection, and get it back on track for healing. Dr. Sweet reminded me I was strong, to not give up, and that he would get me through this. All of a sudden, my concerns dissipated. He always knew how to keep me calm.

When he finished, Tiffany came into the room to wrap my leg. Because she was as close to me as Dr. Sweet, we told her what happened. She let us know that when he came out of my room, he was a basket case. Dr. Sweet was a professional and didn't let emotions get in the way of treatment. But he had traveled a long road with me—almost a year and a half at this point—and wanted the best for me. When I said earlier that he has a passion for his patients, this response is proof positive. He knew by looking at my knee there was likely infection and another surgery would be needed. Tiffany told him he needed to take a walk, see another patient, and get it together. That explained the long wait we had before he returned to do the wound culture. If I had any doubt Dr. Sweet was my ride-or-die, that moment removed it all.

Going through the last 17 months was very traumatic, but it led to developing deep connections with some of my caretakers and doctors. No one would ever dream of the bond one could have with a doctor. Early on, I had designated him my "ride-or-die," and throughout this journey, the comfort I felt with him as my advocate was unexplainable. Dr. Sweet was like my little brother who would fight tigers for me. It isn't often you find a doctor so passionate about his patients that he gets in the battle with you.

The washout surgery was scheduled for April 20. Dr. Sweet would clean out the knee to ensure there was no major infection and reclose the incision in hopes it would heal properly. I can't emphasize enough how each surgery brought on more trauma. Experiencing surgeries continuously for almost a year and a half brings a severe emotional response. I would put on the brave face, but I was pushing down the trauma I was feeling every time another surgery was needed. This would be Surgery #7. The surgery went well, and I was put on a wound vac. It was a large vacuum that helped promote healing but was also attached to an IV pole, so it went with me everywhere. Sometimes, I would have an IV going, and the wound vac and IV tubing would be dancing around me as I navigated my way to physical therapy. A ball and chain seemed less restricting than this contraption.

I would also require rehab after this surgery. After my last experience, I dreaded going to rehab and fretted about where I would end up—it wouldn't be where I had been previously. I requested an evaluation to determine if I could go to the inpatient rehab at Baptist Hospital, where I had my surgery. Baptist Hospital was home to me, and I'd heard glowing reviews about their inpatient rehab services. My caseworker wasn't sure if I'd qualify, but she'd try.

An occupational and physical therapist came to talk to me and evaluate my ability to go through inpatient rehab. Each weekday, I would do three hours of therapy. Could I endure it? Surely I could. Then an admitting nurse from rehab came to talk to me. She was delightful! Her words were encouraging and gave me hope that this was a possibility.

On April 28, I was moved to inpatient rehab at the hospital! This seemed like such a blessing at the time, and in retrospect, I can't imagine being anywhere else. When I arrived in my room, everyone that walked in greeted me with "Welcome to Baptist Rehab!" I felt safe. I felt cared for. I felt like I was home.

The rigorous therapy schedule started the next day. Wake up call was at 7 am when they would bring your breakfast. Along with breakfast came a little sheet with your day's schedule. Every weekday consisted of an hour and a half of PT and then an hour and a half of OT. Physical therapy was intended to help you become mobile and increase your strength to get up and down from chairs and in and out of bed. Occupational therapy was intended to help you do your daily living activities—bathing, brushing your teeth, going to the bathroom—all things we take for granted. Along with those tasks, OT would also help build upper body strength with weight training. In addition, I would have recreational therapy three days a week for 30 minutes. For those sessions, I would get to play games to help keep my mind sharp and active. That sounded like fun!

You were assigned therapists that would be your OT and PT during your entire stay. When I was assigned those therapists, I had no idea how God would bond us, not just for this stay but also for the future stays I would have. To this day, I still keep in close contact with them.

My OT's name was Connie. You always need to love your OT because she sees you at your worst (and at your "naked-est"). Strong and compassionate is how I would describe Connie, and we immediately bonded. She was such an advocate for me. For example, my original room was very small, and she made sure I got moved to a bigger room. As I mentioned earlier, I came with baggage. Literally. The wound vac and IV would often run due to the IV antibiotics I was on. Trying to navigate all of that in my small room was a supreme challenge. As a mover and a shaker, Connie made things happen, and by the afternoon, I was whisked away to a bigger room with a bigger window!

My PT's name was Laura. She and I became fast friends. Her humor was so similar to mine—dad jokes with a sprinkle of corny. As a fellow single, never-married woman, Laura and I bonded, which allowed me to build trust with her. I felt comfortable with her very quickly and felt like she took my overachieving spirit and reined it in as necessary while still utilizing it for my good.

The goal of my stay was to progress to a point where I could function at home. My wound vac and IV sidekick made exercise a challenge, and I usually required extra help from Danny, the PT tech, to keep things moving as I walked. Strengthening my legs was the key to victory.

Aside from the fun of getting bathed and dressed in the mornings, OT consisted of lots of strength training. I did arm weights and the arm bike. The dreaded arm bike. It was a great workout but, whew, it was exhausting. Picture yourself riding a bike, but your arms are doing the work your legs would do. Despite it, I loved being in the gym, talking to people, and getting to know the other therapists. The whole crew was great.

No question, recreational therapy was my favorite! I got to play games with my therapist, Tayler, like Scrabble, Phase 10, and Skip-Bo. Normally, you were in a group for rec therapy, but since COVID, that had changed. I told Tayler how much I loved crafts, and she mentioned doing diamond art painting. I had heard of it but had never done it. Knowing I was a Disney fan, she brought a Mickey and Minnie Mouse kit for me to work on when I was in my room! I was so excited to have something to occupy my time, especially on the weekends when I didn't have PT or OT.

This rehab experience was far better than the experience with my first rehab. The torn patella tendon and healing incision aside, the staff here were so attentive and seemed to really care about my well-being. Having so much therapy each day gave me purpose. Being on this journey kept me away from the busy lifestyle I had before November 2019. I longed for purpose. Doing an hour or so of daily therapy just didn't cut it. Here, I had a full day during the week that kept me from being sequestered in my room alone, ruminating on how much I wanted to be back in the game of life.

My incision was beginning to heal…all except a small pinhole area next to the incision. Dr. Sweet made multiple visits to me in rehab to check on the healing process and reinforce that little spot. He tried stitches and glue, but it still wasn't cooperating. I would likely go home before it healed, and I began to dread that my leg still wasn't healing properly. Dr. Sweet explained that the muscles from tearing the patella tendon had not had time to strengthen, and given the extensiveness of two surgeries so close together, the knee wasn't strong enough to keep the area closed.

Discouraging news seemed to follow me. For once, I wished I would hear, "Wow, you are doing great and healing up perfectly!" It seemed that I would never get to rehab my knee. I convinced myself that this was so minor and it would eventually heal; I just needed to be patient. But, I was on month 18 of this journey and growing weary of playing medical bingo and winning at coverall.

By the end of May, I was projected to go home on June 1. This was the day after Memorial Day, and I was ready to get home, get healed, and soon get on my feet. I imagined my right leg had to be weak since I hadn't used it much since the day I tore my patella tendon. But, rehab for my knee would continue to be delayed until my incision had completely healed and Dr. Sweet felt it could bear the bending of the knee for rehab.

When I left rehab that day, I would miss all those I'd met, but I was ready to take on the summer with a healing knee and a future of exercising back to life.

Chapter Twenty-Five

June 2021

———— ·•●•· ————

Once again, Paige became my caregiver upon arriving home. I set up my main location in my bedroom recliner, complete with books, crafts, and the television remote close by. Oh, and a phone charger. You need that when the majority of your life is spent using your phone.

Due to the nature of my recovery and the end goal—healing—I tried to stay in my room as much as possible with my leg propped up, not walking around too much. That's always a recipe for healing, so I needed to get serious. I was done with this holding pattern and wanted to be as obedient as possible.

Psalm 46:10 came to my mind often. In many translations, it is quoted as, "Be still and know that I am God." But in the Christian Standard Bible, it reads like this, "Stop fighting, and know that I am God." Stop fighting. That's what I was doing. I was fighting against the struggle and just frustrated with my circumstances. I needed to be still *and* stop fighting, though that lesson was slow in seeping into my soul.

As always, Paige was simply the best. We would think of ways to make my life easier after she left, which included having a snack basket by my recliner so that if I got hungry between breakfast and dinner, I would have something to eat. More than anything, her presence brought feelings of safety and calm. She'd been here to help me before, and her return visit made going home with limited mobility much easier.

After Paige left, I was nervous about being at home alone, but I didn't let on to anyone here in Louisville. I needed to be a brave little soldier. I'd been through so much already, so why was being at home alone scary? I believe I lived in the mindset that something bad would happen. Over the course of the past 18 months, my life had been a rollercoaster of medical issues. What if I fell and tore something else? I lived between the past and the not-yet, entangled in emotions that I didn't understand. So I suppressed them - I didn't want to utter them out loud.

Home health came to assist with my care at home. Nursing came three times a week to change my dressing. Physical therapy came to consult with me, but they realized that until I got the all-clear from Dr. Sweet to start rehab, there was no point in them coming. My therapist was named Lee Ann and was so sweet and encouraging. Occupational therapy came, but since I wasn't cleared for showers yet, there wasn't much they could do either. Nursing was the only key to getting me healed and back in action.

Along with home health, I saw Dr. Sweet weekly. He wanted to keep an eye on my knee and monitor the healing. This journey wasn't one I was walking alone. He had been there through every step with me. I knew he deeply wanted to see me recover completely as much as I did. I had come to realize he was passionate about his patients, and I had become his favorite.

From our weekly appointments, he wasn't seeing much improvement in that pinhole. One week he chose to stitch it up in the office. Being the tough girl I am, he numbed me up and went to work. I wouldn't want to be awake or aware of many medical procedures like that, but if I had to choose, his office was less traumatic than the hospital.

By the next week, that stitch had busted open. He decided to do surgery to try to open the pinhole bigger in order to cause a bigger area where the stitching would be more secure. My immediate response was, "SURGERY!?" Dr. Sweet assured me that this would be outpatient and wouldn't take more than 10 minutes. I breathed a sigh of relief, and we got it on the books.

Surgery #8 was on June 24, and Beth chauffeured me to the hospital. Since this was outpatient surgery, I wasn't as nervous as I could have been. Beth promised me Chick-fil-A for breakfast when I was done, so I just kept my eye on the prize.

We got checked in, and I enjoyed seeing all my old friends at pre-op. Dr. Sweet came into my holding room, made his RASII (a monogram) mark on my knee, and we were soon off to the races. I was wheeled into the operating room—the coldest room on the planet—and saw Dr. Sweet and the anesthesia team. I was ready. It wasn't long, and I was out.

The procedure went well except for a snafu with anesthesia. Although to this day I've never been told exactly what happened, I presume that something unexpected happened with intubation, even with the team being briefed on my previous history. Dr. Sweet was rattled when he told Beth how things went, but he accomplished what he needed to do. What started as a small procedure ended up causing a bruise under my chin from ear to ear and shaving years off my surgeon's life. For all the trouble this surgery was, I was hoping "eight is enough," and this would be the last surgery I'd need for a very long time.

Chapter Twenty-Six

July 2021 - September 2021

———··•◆·•··———

"**W**hat did you do on your summer vacation?" I sat in a recliner, waiting for my leg to heal. Sadly, that traumatic 10-minute outpatient procedure didn't work. It wasn't long after surgery that the stitch busted open and we were back to square one. Dr. Sweet was baffled, so he talked to other colleagues and decided to try a portable wound vac.

My home health nurse wanted me to go to a wound doctor. I wasn't keen on the idea of adding another doctor to the mix. Retelling my story yet again was traumatic, and I was getting weary on this journey that was just a few months shy of two years. I didn't want to fall into that pit again, but I was teetering on the edge. Dr. Sweet felt like the wound vac would be a good option, so we tried it.

Wound care actually came to Dr. Sweet's office in the form of a rep from the wound vac manufacturer to see if it would help to close up my wound. The wound vac representative felt his product could help in my specific case. The rep was from a company that didn't have their product available to the Baptist Hospital network due to competitors providing a similar solution. He was good at his job. He was giving it all he had to convince Dr. Sweet to help him get in the door at the hospital instead of focusing on the reason he was there…me. Finally, as the sales manager I used to be, I had to intervene. The rep finally said, "What can I do to get into Baptist?" I intercepted his question and replied, "If this heals my wound, you'll have a voice in Dr. Sweet, but until then, he can't help you."

Man, it felt good to work my sales muscles again! Thankfully, Dr. Sweet didn't say a word against me. He apparently agreed with me, and I realized we worked great as a team. I shouldn't be surprised because as much as he knew me, I felt like I knew him and how he would respond to my deal with the sales rep.

Over the next couple of weeks, I wore a machine like a cross-body purse everywhere I went as it was tethered to my knee. The idea of a wound vac, whether portable or in-patient, is to pull out drainage and provide an environment for healing. My portable vac would often make sounds like a pig. I decided to call her Prevena Pig, as Prevena was the brand name. If I'm going to have this thing with me at all times, I might as well give it a name.

After the portable wound vac saga, I still wasn't healed. It would look better, and then it would get worse. I kept thinking that surely the wound would eventually heal. I hid my emotions during this season. I was sick of hospitals and being discouraged, and I feared that I would end up back in the hospital again. These thoughts were top-of-mind, though I would only mention them in a joking way. Deep down, I knew all these failed attempts only meant one thing…hospitalization.

The thought of meeting with a wound doctor did cross my mind more now. When I mentioned it to Dr. Sweet, he wasn't convinced that it would work. He believed something was at play, keeping the knee from healing. He had removed some internal stitches when he performed the outpatient surgery that he felt was impeding my healing. Those were from the patella tendon repair and would eventually dissolve, but since they were potentially causing a problem, out they came.

There is a phrase that makes me shudder every time I hear it…"you've got this!" I'm not sure when my distaste for this phrase started, but I do know it was before this journey. The phrase implies that I can do anything and overcome any obstacle. That's not true or biblical. During the last few months, I began saying, "God's got this." It was much more accurate and to stay on this road, I needed the reminder. I even found a bracelet with the phrase and began to wear it every day. I had to focus on God or I would not make it through this still following Him.

At the end of September, I celebrated another birthday confined to my home...waiting. In September 2020, I was waiting for clearance to have my knee replacement surgery. A year later, I was still waiting for that knee to heal. Although my countenance didn't show it, I just didn't understand what God was doing. Each morning was a struggle for me to get up and have any kind of purpose. I couldn't work. I couldn't serve fully at church. I felt like my life had no purpose.

During my confinement at home, I would push myself to reach out to others during my day to give me purpose. I was blessed with many people who would help me out at home and bring food. But when they left, I felt very much alone. I made a commitment to reach out to various ladies in my BFG at church. Although I wasn't there in person, I attended via Zoom. I would pray down the list of requests emailed out each week and let them know I was praying for them. I would do it for everyone, whether they knew me or not. It was a way to serve and to begin to connect with people I didn't know.

What did the future hold? This question haunted me daily. I didn't want to lose my life. I still ached to go back to the way things had been. I knew I had no actual job to return to since I was employed by name only after my division had been sold, and as each passing month went by, I felt as though I was further and further away from the life I remembered. I didn't understand how anything good could come of this journey—I had just lost time. As discouraged as I was, the journey was about to get even more interesting.

Chapter Twenty-Seven

October 2021 - November 2021

My knee continued its pendulum swing: healing up, breaking down, healing up again. As I changed the dressing daily, I wasn't convinced the treatments used were helping. I was discouraged and felt impending doom on its way. Sherrie, my home health nurse, became so special to me. We bonded quite a bit, and I knew she had my best interest at heart. One day when she came to do the dressing change and check things out, she had a concerned look on her face. I questioned her immediately, and she shared that she was concerned my wound was infected. She called Dr. Sweet to get orders for a wound culture. The impending doom I felt was happening.

In a couple of days, the home-health wound nurse arrived to culture my wound. She informed me that it would take a few days for the culture results to come back because it took time for it to produce whatever bacteria—if any—was growing. I got a lump in my stomach and was convinced the wound was likely infected. I knew that would mean going to the hospital and getting a spacer in my knee. I'd already been down the infected-joint rodeo and knew if this was infected, the spacer and rehab were in my future.

At this point, I was numb. I hadn't gotten the results back yet, but my gut feeling was that my knee was infected. Whenever I felt this way—and it happened a lot on this journey—I just wanted to sleep. Closing my eyes, taking a nap, and forgetting about my problems was always my solution to a problem. If nothing else, it was my escape mechanism.

All the fears I had from the last two years came flooding over me. I couldn't reconcile what was happening in my mind. Hadn't I been through enough? Wasn't there a limit to my suffering? I began to search my heart but had no energy left to even think. Could I fight this battle much longer? After tossing around every scenario I could think of, I knew I had to do the next right thing. And that was to keep doing what I was doing every day—wait. I loathed that four-letter word. Wait.

It was during this time of waiting that God did an enormous work in my heart. From the beginning of this journey almost two years ago, my prayer had been that I would quickly heal and get back to work and back to my life. I kept thinking this time was just a small blip that I'd work through and then return to my regularly-scheduled programming. But that wasn't God's plan. That was my plan. And as much as I had kept praying and focusing on that goal, God was working to prepare me for a whole new life—one that would look nothing like the life I had before November 2019.

As I waited, feeling as though I knew that hospitalization was imminent, I prayed a prayer I'll never forget.

> *Lord, for the last 23 months, I've prayed that You would bring me out of this situation and return me back to life. And it hasn't happened. I don't know why. I may never know why. But I'm exhausted. So, I'm praying what I believe I need to pray right now. Father, help me to surrender completely to You in this situation. Whatever the coming days bring, give me the strength to face them. I'm weary and worn down. And I'm tired of praying for what has obviously been my will. Let me surrender to Yours.*

That prayer was one I should have prayed long before 23 months into this journey. But, I'm human, and I find myself in the driver's seat of my life more often than not. The Lord had used my broken spirit to draw me to Him even more. I had no idea how this prayer would be the catalyst for so much more that was about to happen to me, or how the next few months would actually be the worst months of my life.

The culture came back, and it was positive for infection. I contacted Dr. Sweet, and he put me on an antibiotic. I also made an appointment for October 6. I dreaded this appointment, knowing what I expected to be the outcome. Beth took me and was still very positive that I wouldn't need hospitalization. I kept trying to convince her that I did, and she assumed it was my negative, broken spirit overreacting.

When Dr. Sweet saw the knee, he had the exact diagnosis I had assumed—an antibiotic spacer had to be placed so that we could get rid of the infection. As Beth countered with her solutions, tears rolled down her face. She was hurting so much for me. This friend and sister had been on every step of this journey, and she was broken and tired, too. Dr. Sweet and I both assured her this was what had to be done. I didn't cry because I was expecting to hear that the resolution for this infection meant another surgery, and I was fresh off of a prayer that was turning my heart toward complete surrender to God. Dr. Sweet hugged her and me, and off we went to begin this next act in the play.

We left the appointment with orders that we'd head to the hospital upon a call that the bed was ready. With an infection, immediate admission is easy. Surgery would occur the next day and, like always, Beth would be there. We got the call and then headed to Taco Bell for my "last meal" before admission. I had no idea how long this admission would be, but I remember eating my comfort food in the parking lot of the hospital, not knowing this would be the last time I'd breathe fresh air in 2021.

Being back on the ortho floor of the hospital was like walking into the Cheers bar. The nurses and aides hugged me and welcomed me back, making this much more tolerable than it could have been. I was ready to tackle this next surgery and move forward. I knew what life would be like recovering with a spacer, and I wasn't looking forward to that, but if I could stay in rehab through the extent of my IV treatment and go right back to surgery for my new knee replacement (which would now be necessary after the spacer was put in and taken out), I could make it.

The next day, I went down to pre-op and was greeted again like an old friend—which I was becoming at that point. Dr. Sweet came in to mark my knee, and I was ready to get this party started…again. My last surgery, which was outpatient, had an unpleasant outcome due to the intubation issue. I reminded Dr. Sweet and the anesthesiologist of that event so as to equip them not to let *that* happen again.

Surgery #9 went fine, and I was soon back in my room recovering. By the next day, physical therapy had started. I was restricted to toe-touch weight bearing, as you can't ever put full weight on a spacer. That was a challenge, but I was able to accomplish this easier than I expected. The Lord was really strengthening my upper body, and that would be very handy much later.

One of my PTs, Sarah, was the daughter-in-law of a PT I'd had before, Jenny. I loved Jenny, and she knew Beth from connections between their children. Sarah was equally as good, and she was also a believer. Though I couldn't do much at first, Sarah never failed to cheer me on. One day she was there for one of my sessions while I watched the live stream of the Kentucky Baptist Convention Women's Conference. Jaylynn was the speaker, and I just knew I would be there in the front row in other circumstances, but God had other plans. Instead, I was able to watch the sessions on my phone. While it was playing, Sarah was there working with me. And during that part of Jaylynn's session, she mentioned me and the journey I'd been on over the last 23 months. My heart so wanted to be among the ladies of my church and to support Jaylynn, but God's plan meant otherwise. Sarah could tell I was emotional and was so gracious to allow me to take a break from our exercises.

It wasn't long after my surgery that I was slated to go to rehab. Thankfully, I was able to return to Baptist Rehab. Given all the complications from my knee surgery and infection, I was allowed to qualify again. Like the ortho floor, it was great to be reunited once again with the team that was so caring toward me. I was assigned again Laura and Connie as my PT and OT, so we could pick right up where we left off.

As I worked in the rehab gym each day, I noticed quite a few amputees. I was amazed at how well they did and stayed so upbeat. Forrest was my favorite! He was a boisterous, fun-loving guy who was a below-knee amputee. He used eight-pound weights as opposed to my one- or two-pound weights, so I was impressed with his strength. And he kept a bottle of hot sauce in his room to "spice" up the hospital food. I feel ya, Forrest. It surely needed something.

What impressed me the most was his positive outlook. Forrest knew he'd eventually lose his other leg below the knee, yet he was always cracking jokes and epitomized joy. Shame engulfed me as I was here with both legs, yet I was so discouraged at times. What if I lost my leg like Forrest? I quickly pushed that out of my mind, thinking that it only happens to people who have accidents or who are diabetic. He made an impression on me to keep the right perspective.

My social worker, Susan, was working hard to keep me in rehab until Dr. Sweet cleared me for my knee replacement surgery. Going home in between was frightening since I couldn't put weight on my leg. How would I take care of myself? We seemed to have made it work with insurance to keep me there, so I held my breath. I hadn't felt well for a few days, waking up congested and just feeling blah. I mentioned it to Connie and my nurse, who told Dr. Gormley, my rehab doctor - and a COVID test was ordered. I was sure it wasn't COVID. I'd been vaccinated and hadn't been anywhere except the hospital and rehab. But when the results came back, I was positive for Covid.

Mark off "COVID" on my medical bingo card. I knew COVID was still a reality, but I had been so sequestered and masked when I left my room that I truly thought I could avoid the virus. I lived through this pandemic for so long before I finally succumbed to it myself. It was likely the Delta variant, and I was soon packed up and sent to the COVID unit of the hospital. I was immediately quarantined, and all rehab staff had to come into my room for my therapies with their hazmat gear.

In the COVID unit of the hospital, the entire staff looked like astronauts. The spacesuit they had to wear came with its own ventilation system. There was an air purifier in my room, and attendants only came in my room when I needed actual physical assistance or they needed to take vitals. Otherwise, they cracked open my door and asked if I was okay or needed anything. When Dr. Sweet suited up to come in and see me, I said, "You aren't surprised that I have COVID now, are you?" He shook his head in disbelief as I continued to play medical bingo-winning coverall.

My infectious disease doctor, Dr. Klausing, who was treating me with IV antibiotics, was able to get me the antibodies infusion to help combat the virus. The only symptoms I had were terrible congestion, fatigue (which could have also been from surgery recovery), and an unbelievable craving for orange juice. I'm sure no one has reported an orange juice craving as an actual symptom of COVID, but I'm here to validate its existence. I couldn't get enough of that nectar! I was drinking it nonstop. I'm sure the vitamin C was helping, but I was keeping my aides hopping, bringing me cups of it day and night.

My physical therapy continued even on the COVID floor. Thankfully, Sarah had been assigned to my unit! She would gear up and work with me and said I was doing really well. She also had a magic touch for making me milkshakes! As is no surprise, hospital food isn't top-shelf quality. When she asked if I would like a milkshake, I jumped at that delicacy. Sarah had perfected the ability to take the ice cream cups and cartons of milk and mix them together to create the most delicious milkshake. She would bring me one almost daily, and I enjoyed seeing her as much as the treat.

I had to stay in the COVID unit for ten days before being released. I entered on November 11, and Dr. Sweet planned my surgery for November 24. According to Dr. Klausing and Dr. Sweet, I would be cleared for my new knee. Once I completed my obligatory COVID quarantine, I moved to the ortho floor to prepare for surgery. My nomadic life in the Baptist facility continued as I moved back to the ortho floor on November 21. The last few weeks had been a blur, and I barely knew it was getting close to the holidays, yet I was about to have surgery the day before Thanksgiving. My mind flashed back to Thanksgiving 2020. I was home and able to travel to Lancaster, Kentucky, to have Thanksgiving dinner with my friends Karen, Alisa (Karen's sister), Bobby (Alisa's husband), and Mary (Karen and Alisa's mom), along with people from Alisa and Bobby's church. I could walk into Alisa and Bobby's home with some assistance and it felt amazing. This year, I'd be spending it in the hospital again. Was my life going to be a continuum of regression? I remembered I needed to surrender that to the Lord.

Surgery #10 went fine, and I was hopeful that after a few days, I would head back to rehab. I couldn't wait to get moving with my new knee, which hadn't seen action since before my patella tendon was torn. Soon after surgery, PT started while I was still in the hospital, and merely moving from the bed to the chair caused massive bleeding that was incredible. Blood was everywhere, and I knew that couldn't be good. Each time they attempted to get me out of bed, my leg would spew blood. Literally. During one episode, the blood was shooting out like a fountain, and my nurse was a target. Nurses would come in and rewrap my leg, and we would end our PT session early. Something was causing my leg to bleed, and bleed a lot.

The last attempt to get out of bed was so bad that I felt dizzy and faint from blood loss. The nurse told me to lie back as clearly my blood pressure was dropping. After that incident, I was instructed not to get out of bed again.

This couldn't be a good sign, and I feared what was to come. When Dr. Sweet rounded the next time, he told me that my incision wasn't holding together. Unfortunately, my patella tendon was so weak after repair that it wasn't strong enough to hold my skin together to heal. He told me the best option would be to do a muscle flap procedure. The surgery would take part of my calf muscle and pull it around to cover my knee in an effort to reinforce the area to hold my incision together.

This was not the solution I wanted to hear. Dr. Sweet had considered this surgery early in the summer when my incision wasn't healing at first, and it sounded pretty extreme. My right leg was already compromised with rheumatoid arthritis, and I wasn't keen on having my muscles twisted like tree trunks. But I knew that this wasn't going to heal in the current condition. Surgery #11 was in my future.

Dr. Sweet informed me that this was not his specialty but that his colleague, Dr. Foeger, would be doing the procedure. My heart skipped a beat, and it must have shown on my face because without me taking a breath, Dr. Sweet said he would be with him for the surgery. I'm sure my sigh was visible. In the ten previous surgeries, he was my ride-or-die. I didn't want to face this surgery without him in there.

I thought back to my prayer earlier in the month when I released my future to God's plans, not mine. Praying that prayer seemed to have made things worse, not better. I asked God why and wondered if I maybe shouldn't have ever prayed that prayer—like it was an invitation to God to see how much I could actually endure. At this point, I had been in and out of the hospital for almost two years, had ten surgeries (and prepping for the 11th), and still had not recovered enough to resume my life fully. My prayer of surrender was my white flag that I was tired of fighting to get back to my life. I had to keep focused on that prayer when I felt my life crumbling and slowly falling deeper into the pit where I had been before.

Chapter Twenty-Eight

December 2021

⸱⸱●⸱⸱

The day was approaching for Surgery #11—the muscle flap surgery for my knee wound that just wouldn't stay closed. I wasn't keen on having this procedure, but I knew that my incision wasn't healing. Since this incision was literally a bloody mess after my knee replacement, it was a necessity.

Once again, I headed to pre-op as I encountered all the same questions and routines from the ten times before. Dr. Sweet marked my knee, even though Dr. Foeger would be doing the actual procedure. I appreciated Dr. Sweet protected me to ensure I was getting the best care. I felt loved and more than just another patient.

After surgery, I had a wound vac placed on the incision that would stay on for ten days. Dr. Foeger made it clear to the nursing staff that he would be the one to remove the wound vac when it was time. I was all too familiar with wound vacs, so this wasn't anything new for me. My skin graft was minimal and didn't hurt, nor did my knee. I prayed everything would seal up nicely.

On Sunday, December 12, Dr. Foeger came in to remove the wound vac. When he did, I didn't like the sound he made, and it turns out I was on to something. This wasn't my first disappointment post-surgery. Even behind the mask, I knew that Dr. Foeger wasn't pleased with what he saw as he looked at my knee. The incision had dehisced, and there was a hematoma on top. In layman's terms, the wound had not closed with the wound vac but opened up even more, and a large blood clot was resting on top. He quickly said, "There's nothing else we can do but amputate." The bottom fell out of my stomach. "Amputate?! I've been battling healing this leg for months, and now I'm going to lose it. How was this possible?" There had to be more that could be done. I didn't want to give up after two years of fighting for this leg. I didn't say a thing but thought, *I need to talk to Dr. Sweet. He won't give up on me.* Surely there was a way to save my leg. We haven't come this far for things to end like this. I was convinced this was all a bad dream. Maybe the anesthesia hadn't worn off yet? Looking back, I was in shock and denial. I had encountered wound vacs before that didn't work. Maybe the wound vac wasn't the answer. I wanted to keep fighting. Dr. Foeger didn't know my full case. He didn't know that I was a fighter and battled the odds. Surely amputation was not the only answer.

Dr. Sweet came to talk to me, and it was a tender moment. I'll never forget what he said: "I'm so sorry it has come to this." My knee wasn't healing, no matter what we did, and amputation was the solution to move forward with life. But he didn't want me to make the decision right away. He recommended I talk to other doctors before agreeing to the amputation. His recommendation was Dr. Yakanti, who did my very first surgery. He said if he were facing this decision, Dr. Yakanti would be first on his list. I agreed to talk to him, and Dr. Sweet gave me time and space. This news was a lot to process.

When Dr. Yakanti came, he was very thorough about my options. To save the leg would likely require two more years and four more surgeries. With the damage to my patella tendon and the weakness due to the repair, there was no guarantee that I could walk on that leg again. And given how the other efforts to save the leg turned out, I may lose my leg anyway. Otherwise, I could amputate now and move on with life. It seemed like a no-brainer decision, but at the same time, it was hard to fathom. I so wanted to save my leg, but I didn't want to spend two more years in hospitals and rehab enduring more surgeries. Hearing that I may not walk again on my leg and that amputation could be the end result was disheartening. I knew I couldn't mentally handle what I'd already suffered for even longer. My heart was sad, but I knew amputation was inevitable if I had any chance to resume life again.

Dr. Yakanti said many above-the-knee amputees, which is what I would be, don't walk again. Without hesitation, I boldly said, "Oh, Dr. Yakanti, I will walk again." Walking was really the only goal I had over these two years. Even if that meant walking with a prosthetic, I could learn how to navigate life. I'm a fighter, and I was determined I would walk again.

Once I was set on amputation, I wanted to talk to Dr. Gormley. He was the medical director of rehab and also oversaw the amputee clinic. He explained the process and timeline. I don't remember much of what he said, but I followed along and felt like moving forward with the amputation was something I could do. Dr. Gormley suggested I talk with Chris Luckett of Louisville Prosthetics. He would be able to explain what to expect from the prosthetic process.

Chris came to talk with me, and I loved him from the start. He was very upbeat about the prosthetic process and stressed that their goal was to get folks up and walking. Beth was with me when he came, and she asked him if he'd ever had any RA patients before. Beth knows me so well. She knows what I'm thinking and asks those questions that I'm afraid to ask. Part of me didn't want to hear an answer that didn't have a positive outcome. A person with RA has limited mobility, even with all of their limbs. Their joints are typically compromised, and they experience chronic pain with mobility. Given that was a norm for me, could I actually function with a prosthetic? Chris said he had RA patients and saw many folks with complications walk again. That was great news to me. It didn't take away the sadness of what I was going through, but it seemed like a tender mercy from God.

Dr. Sweet scheduled the surgery for December 31. By the time I had talked to multiple people and made the decision to amputate, it was mere days before Christmas. He was going out of town for the holiday but would be back to do the surgery. I asked him if he was sure he could do the surgery. He, of course, said yes. I asked him again so that he would understand I was more concerned about him emotionally doing this surgery than the mere ability to do the surgery. He had fought beside me for this knee with me for two years. Having to perform an amputation on a leg he had surgically tried to improve for so long couldn't have been easy. Dr. Sweet kept his game face on and assured me he could do it. After all we had been through to get the knee in working order, this outcome seemed somewhat like a defeat. Ever the professional, he never wavered in his responses.

Since my muscle flap surgery on December 3rd, I hadn't felt well in general. I had no appetite and just felt nauseous. I hardly ate breakfast and only about four or five bites at other meals. Friends would bring food, but even then, I could only stomach a few bites. I couldn't pinpoint why I felt this way, but I literally lost interest in eating. I assumed my emotional state had my physical body in distress. I tried to embrace the reality of losing my leg, and it felt like it took every cell in my body to wrap my head around these unfortunate circumstances.

Life without a limb would mean my life would never be the same. I prayed that I would be able to walk again, but like in everything I'd experienced, there were no guarantees. Adaptations would have to be made to my home, and losing my right leg meant driving my car would require hand controls. Not understanding all that would come with being an amputee was a blessing. I couldn't have taken it all in and processed what it would look like post-amputation. Even being able to look at myself without a leg and accepting that it was me was beyond my comprehension. The prayer of surrender was still in my mind as I realized how much I did have to surrender to get through this next step.

My dressing was changed twice a day during each shift, and thirty minutes before the dressing change, I would receive pain meds. I'm not normally a pain-med kind of girl, but they insisted, due to the pain it caused in my knee to change the dressing. The muscle flap surgery had reconstructed my calf muscle, and my nerves hadn't caught up. When they worked on the dressing, I'd feel it in my ankle. It was quite strange. I never wanted to look at it because I knew the wound was bad. Nurses had said you could see the knee implant, which indicated how open this wound was. This was more evidence that the muscle flap surgery didn't strengthen my muscles and confirmed that amputation was probably the best route.

On Christmas Day, sweet twin girls from my church, Sarah and Rebekah, brought chicken enchiladas and ate with me. Again, I couldn't eat much, but I tried my best to get down as much as I could. I attributed my lack of appetite and feeling unwell to emotional stress. I was losing my leg. A leg I had fought for over the past two years. I'm not a quitter, so I felt somewhat like a failure. Where did things go so wrong? Was it during the summer when my pinhole wouldn't heal? I constantly replayed the last six months, wondering what I could have done differently. It consumed my thoughts. I had no desire to engage with people and felt physically unwell. Though I had logically accepted and planned my amputation, I emotionally had not processed this change in plans. This wasn't how God was supposed to show up! He was supposed to save my leg for His glory. Where is the glory to God in this outcome? I discovered no answers. Outside of this not going according to my plan, I was fearful for what the future meant for me. Could I live alone? I had a very independent life, and now I wondered how I could live without a leg. I knew many amputees lived full lives, and I was tenacious and resilient enough to think I could do the same. I blocked out thinking through what my life would actually look like after amputation. I would start to think about driving again and going back to work full-time, but when I did, I stopped myself. I didn't want to admit that those things either wouldn't happen for a long time or maybe not at all. Even with my denial of what the future could hold, I knew this was my path, and I prayed God would help me embrace this new life and see how He might work through this massive loss.

I also thought much about my mom. She was a below-knee amputee due to her diabetes. I remember when she lost her leg - she seemed to manage well. Her amputation wasn't long after my first hip replacement when I was 28. Due to her diabetes, she had battled ongoing infections in her toes, foot, and then her leg. My mom was as tough as they come, and she knew that to live, she would have to lose her leg. In some ways, I was in the same predicament. She was able to walk with a walker, then a cane, so I felt if she could do it, so could I. She was 64 when she lost her leg, even older than I was. I remembered her prosthetic and how she got around. I dwelled on those thoughts to grasp my own reality. I struggled with all the unknowns and the journey to come since I'd already traveled a road that had lasted two years. I wasn't ready to admit that I was going to become an amputee. I wasn't in the mood for people to tell me how God would use me in so many ways as an amputee. I felt broken down physically and emotionally. I so wished my mom was here to help me through this time in my life. Maybe she would have some great insight to share with me, to make me somewhat hopeful for my future.

On December 26, I don't remember much. I remember dietary bringing my breakfast, and I ignored it once again. Outside of that, I just slept. I didn't feel good and didn't have the energy to keep my eyes open. I didn't have pain, but I was just very sad about how things were turning out for me. When I was depressed, sleeping was my escape. I found out later I had two visitors, Harlene and Heather, from my BFG. When they arrived, I was asleep, so they didn't wake me. Harlene later told me that I looked gray and like I was in a casket.

She was right. That night I coded. I heard later that the nurse came in because my oxygen level had dropped. She said I responded to her question, and then she went to get something and came back in. Once she returned, I was unresponsive. I became one of the "code blues" I'd heard over the loudspeaker so many times before. Those announcements always made me stop and pray for that person. Now I was the person behind a "code blue" announcement.

I came back to consciousness while people were wheeling me somewhere in the hospital. I heard their conversations, which were nothing to do with me but about whatever was going on in their lives. My chest was killing me. I felt like an elephant had stomped on top of me. I gathered enough energy to say, "My chest is hurting." The nurse told me that was because they had to do chest compressions. Whoa. While they were transporting me to who knows where I wondered why I needed chest compressions. Panic swirled around inside me because I had no energy for it to show through my outside actions. I was so weak that I couldn't put together my thoughts or utter any words. I'm sure I had questions, but I couldn't formulate them. Even if I did, my weary soul couldn't take it. My body was so decimated I didn't have any fight in me to push for answers.

We finally got to our location, which I later realized was the ICU. The nurses were busily setting things up, and one nurse finally explained what happened to me. When the nurse on the ortho floor came back to my room, she found me unresponsive and with a blood sugar of ten. A normal blood sugar level is 80 to 100. They had to do chest compressions, but my heart never completely stopped beating. They could have told me my leg was amputated, and I would have had the same response: shock. I didn't know what to say or how to react. I was still so weak that I didn't know if I was thinking clearly. It took everything I had to utter words.

I kept asking for water or ice chips. I was so thirsty. The nurses kept putting me off. I'd wait for what I felt was a fair amount of time and garner up the energy to ask again. Still they put me off. Finally, after I asked for probably the fifteenth time, another nurse came to my bedside and said, "You are not out of the woods yet. Once we get you stable, we'll get you some ice chips." She said it sternly enough to help me realize the danger I was still in. I kept quiet after that and waited for them to provide what I needed.

A doctor came in to put in a central line. I'd had multiple PICC lines before, which were treacherous enough to endure. This central line was even worse. He put it in my neck, and I could tell it was complex. Later, I found out there were three lines coming out of that central line to provide me with the fluids and medications I needed. I had to lie very still, and once it was done, I was glad it was over. The doctor had been conversing with the nurses and joking about things of the day. I didn't find his lightheartedness comforting at all. In fact, I wanted to smack him, but I didn't have the energy. Soon after the central line was put in, I drifted off to sleep, still with no water or ice chips.

The next couple of days were foggy. Beth was coming in from an out-of-town trip when all of this happened. Jaylynn came the next morning to be with me. I don't remember that, but she was there. While texting Beth an update, Jaylynn took a picture of me to show her. It wasn't good. Jaylynn stepped out into the hall to call her husband, Bill. Just a few months prior, Jaylynn had lost her mom after a long battle with dementia and COVID. She told Bill through tears, "I can't do this again." Once again, I was dancing in the valley of the shadow of death, even if I wasn't fully conscious to realize it.

Lots of doctors came to see me—kidney, liver, and vascular—along with my infectious disease doctor. Apparently, my kidneys were shutting down and my liver was malfunctioning. When Jaylynn came to see me one day, I was completely yellow. The nurses let her know that was due to my kidneys failing. There was talk of putting me on dialysis temporarily, but that didn't happen. Right then, the medical staff was trying to determine what issue caused me to be in my current state. Although I knew it was serious since I was in the ICU, I didn't realize the gravity of my situation. I had no energy to ask many questions and didn't pray. When you are that sick, you truly have to depend on the prayers of others because you don't have the capacity to pray at all.

After examinations and tests, none of which I remember, I was told I had ileus. Ileus is a condition where your intestines can't push food through the digestive system. I had a significant GI blockage because of this complication. The amount of opioid pain medication I had taken was the cause. It explained so much—my lack of appetite and my life-threatening blood sugar level. Now, it was time to resolve this problem.

The nursing staff first put a nasogastric tube (NG) through my nose and throat to my stomach. Once the nurses inserted the tube and told me to swallow, I didn't remember anything. I assume I passed out swallowing the tube. I can't swallow a large pill; only by the grace of God could I swallow this tube. Remember, I'm hard to intubate, so inserting this tube felt like a miracle. The NG tube was placed to help decompress my stomach due to the intestinal obstruction. Sometimes they are used for feeding but not in my case. After the tube placement, the nurses began cleaning out the obstruction. I was given Dilaudid, a powerful pain medication, every two hours, so I was not aware of what was going on. The nurses told Beth and Jaylynn it was so bad that the cleansing took all night.

I was zonked out due to all the Dilaudid and from the sheer size of the procedure the staff did. When I finally came around, it felt like I'd been asleep for six days. The nurses came in and asked me what year it was. I stopped to think and said, "2022?" They would say, "Wrong. Try again." Then I said "2021." I seriously thought I'd lived past the New Year. At one point, I even told the nurses I was twenty-two years old.

My mind felt fuzzy. When I was asked a question, I could process the answer but couldn't express it easily. At first I thought I'd had a stroke, but after the nurses' assessment, it was determined I didn't. I was so slow to respond and feeling so out of it, but I also didn't know the extent of how my body was, or wasn't, functioning. There is some sort of blessing in not knowing.

I continued to drift in and out, sleeping for much of the time. When I was awake, I realized who was by my side: Beth, Jaylynn, Bill, Christie, and my other precious friends, Amy and Chad. I heard murmurs while they talked to each other, and although I couldn't hear all they were saying, I had a feeling things weren't good. When my core support group finds themselves at my bedside constantly, it must mean something.

Jaylynn had asked Beth to play praise and worship music. Beth pulled up a playlist on her phone and started the music. When I heard it and realized what was happening, I said, "Blackwell, you play praise and worship music when it's the end." I was being humorous, but in some ways, my statement was serious. As I drifted in and out, I remember Amy being by my bedside. She played music as well and wanted me to sing along. I think I did sing something, but I don't remember what song. Music wasn't helping, and I was convinced my time on Earth was coming to a close.

The activity around me and how I felt weary and exhausted caused me to think about what was truly happening. In my heart, I so assuredly thought this was my time to go. I would go see Jesus and avoid my amputation. That sounded glorious. I couldn't wait to get to Heaven, have my glorified body that would be whole again, and see all my loved ones there. The past two years were tough, and God could take me now and pull me out of this horrible valley.

I told Beth and Jaylynn I was going to see Jesus, and it would be soon. They both responded that it wasn't my decision but God's decision. I didn't waver. I was heading to Heaven soon and ready to go. I can't express the comfort I felt, believing it was the end. That assurance and peace was remarkable. Everyone would claim I was drugged up, but I was thinking clearly. It was time to go. I felt like a burden was lifted, knowing that I would see Jesus soon. If I ever needed assurance of my salvation, this time was affirming the decision I made at the age of eight.

Our senior adult pastor, Larry Buchanan, and his wife, Lettie, came to see me. They had lost their twenty-one-year-old daughter to osteosarcoma in 2018. Her name was Samantha, or Sam, as we called her. When they came to see me, I told them, "I'm going to see Sam soon! I'll give her a big hug!" Larry quickly jumped in to tell me that I would see Sam one day, but not any day soon. My cousin, Wes, came to see me, who is not a follower of Christ. I asked him to read the book of John - to promise me he'd read the book of John. I was executing my last requests any chance I got.

At some point, as Beth tells it, I had raised my hand and was singing, "Precious Lord, Take My Hand." Just as I was singing it, the nurse came in. She grabbed my hand and said, "I'll take your hand, and you're not going anywhere." It's a nurse's job to never give up on a patient. I was not in good shape and could have died, but the staff wasn't going to let me know that could be the outcome or I might have stopped fighting.

According to Beth, I also talked to Paige on the phone at some point, but again, I didn't remember it. I was in and out, but one thing I knew for sure: I was going to Heaven soon. I was conscious enough to feel nervous about that transition, but I looked forward to getting to that destination. The majority of this time prior to my amputation was foggy. I knew I was in the ICU, but I had no real concept of time.

Beth, Paige, and Jaylynn all told me later, much later, that they thought it was very possible and probable I was going to die. They were encouraging to me, but in their hearts, they knew I was very sick. Nobody was sure my body could fight back again. Jaylynn went home and sobbed as Bill held her. She told him that I was ready to die and wanted to die. Bill's response was so on target, "Can you blame her after all she's been through?" He was right. I had all the fight I could take. I didn't want to keep fighting when I knew there was a home waiting for me in Heaven. Beth said she prayed that, although she didn't want to lose me, God would take me home if I couldn't live an independent life. I know that it took bravery to pray that way. Beth had begged God to keep me here two years prior, but she knew I wouldn't want to live on earth if I couldn't be independent. She called Paige and shared with her the prayer, saying she even felt bad praying for God to take me. Paige told her that she had prayed the exact same way that morning. My friends loved me and wanted me to live, but not if my life was going to look like this long-term.

I remember looking at Jaylynn and thinking this was the time. I smiled, closed my eyes, and saw a very bright light. I know many people talk of the bright light they see when they have died and been resuscitated. My heart didn't stop, but I thought for sure this was the pathway leading to Heaven. I felt comforted and at peace and so ready to meet Jesus. I was nervous about the unknown but so anxious to see Heaven and all those I missed terribly… especially my mom and dad.

Shortly after that episode, I awoke and realized I was alive and still in the hospital. I felt so discouraged. I didn't want to be here! Jesus was taking me home; why was I still here? My emotions were all over the place. Beth reminded me that Dr. Sweet was worried about me but would be there to do my amputation surgery. After that statement, I declared to Beth and Christie that I wasn't having surgery. "No surgery!" I kept saying over and over.

I didn't want surgery; I wanted to die. I was ready. Beth told me I needed surgery, and we'd already decided. I repeated again, "No surgery!" Finally, Beth showed me a picture of my leg. It was awful. My leg had become septic, and there was no saving it. I took a deep breath and agreed. I wasn't sure if I would live or die after this surgery, and frankly, I preferred to die. But, if I made it through surgery, I knew I had to fight to keep going. I had surrendered my will to God, and even though I wanted to die, I had to be obedient to His will...even if that meant I would live.

Prior to the surgery, Dr. Sweet came in to see me. He was in street clothes, so I believe it was either late the night before or early the morning of surgery. He said, "I've been so worried about you." That's all I remember. The Lord was gracious because I don't remember much of the time surrounding my my amputation - another one of God's tender mercies.

The only memory from the day of the amputation was during pre-op. The anesthesiologist completed a nerve block on my right leg in preparation for the surgery. I felt like I was in a scene from the old Batman series and being tortured by the Joker. I would feel a shooting pain and scream out. It seemed the doctor didn't care and just kept jolting me. Did he not hear me? Couldn't he stop this torture? I thought, "This leg is coming off; can we not put it through so much before surgery?" I heard the doctor say one of my nerves wasn't responding, and I answered him, "Yes, it is!" Shortly after that, I was out.

For this most dramatic Surgery #12, I remember nothing about pre-op, the operating room, or post-op. That was such a blessing from the Lord. I'm not sure how I would have handled being more aware and remembering all those details vividly. My memory is very good, and this is a memory I wouldn't want to have as a visual reminder.

At some point after surgery, I do remember being back in the ICU. Over the next few days, I became more coherent. The surgery was on Friday, December 31, and I remember on Sunday, January 2, Beth was with me. She was watching our church's live stream, and I could hear some of the music. This time the music didn't bother me. It felt comforting; it was good to have some normalcy happening in the background of my not-so-normal life.

From the moment I got my NG tube, I could not eat or drink. I still had the NG tube, even after surgery. I lived off the fluids and nourishment I was given intravenously and the little sponges drenched in water I could suck on periodically. Those felt like wonderful pillows going in my mouth to keep me from being so dry. I would suck on those sponges until they were bone dry and literally falling apart in my mouth. Then I'd ask for another one. Once I was more awake than asleep, I couldn't handle the dry mouth.

I thought about Jesus on the cross. The soldiers would only give him a sponge filled with wine vinegar to quench His thirst. Once He drank, He bowed His head and said, "It is finished." Then He died. This scene was the perfect combination of Jesus as man and Jesus as God. Like us, he was thirsty as his body was shutting down. Once He drank and declared, "It is finished," He was the God-man fulfilling what would save us all from our sins. I thought how awful that was when I'd suck the life out of a small sponge of water. It made me long for Jesus even more. I still wanted to go home to Heaven. My longing and grieving were far from over.

I was angry about being here on Earth, though I didn't talk about it with others. It was hard to talk with the NG tube and frankly, I didn't want to talk. Nobody would understand how I felt. Everyone was thrilled that I survived dancing in the valley of the shadow of death while I was in the ICU and coming through amputation surgery. I wasn't. I had danced in the valley so many times that I wanted to complete that dance and go to my heavenly home. I felt separated from this world. I should have felt thrilled that I still had breath within me, but I was now minus a leg and longing for Heaven.

Chapter Twenty-Nine

January 2022

———— ·•●•· ————

I moved out of the ICU on January 6 to a step-down unit. I fought the nurse over leaving the ICU. I may be the only human to ever want to stay in intensive care. My concern was leaving the constant care I had and something happening again. My friend, Amy, sat by my side while my nurse compassionately shared that I was moving to a new room because I was better, which was a good thing. I wasn't fully convinced, but I had to move on.

When I arrived in my new room, my NG tube was removed. That was an uncomfortable feeling, especially since I was fully awake and aware when it happened, unlike the original placement of the NG tube. Now that it was gone, I had to begin working on eating and drinking again. Neither activity was appealing to me. A speech therapist came to help me learn to swallow again. After not eating for more than three weeks, I couldn't just pick up eating and drinking again without training.

Small sips of clear fluids were all I could tolerate. My stomach couldn't handle much. My body weight had decreased to a level I hadn't seen since high school or earlier. Somehow that made me happy. I'd lost so much weight, but this wasn't the way to do it, and my body was so weak I couldn't sit up on my own.

Let's not forget I was missing my leg. I would periodically have the phantom pain people talk about—the pain that occurs where there is no longer a limb. It would shoot through my leg like a jolt of electricity and cause me to jump. I had to get used to looking down and not seeing a leg from my thigh down. Honestly, it was hard to look at first. It would take time to grasp the fact that I no longer had a leg.

My days were spent in bed watching the Food Network. In all my months, even years, in the hospital and rehab, I had always watched my phone, never the television. But now things were different. I didn't have the energy to look at my phone. I just mindlessly watched the various cooking competition shows that played over and over.

When I grew weary of focusing on food concoctions, I'd think about Jesus. Why didn't He take me home? I'd recount in my head the story from Mark 5:25-34:

> Now a woman suffering from bleeding for twelve years had endured much under many doctors. She had spent everything she had and was not helped at all. On the contrary, she became worse. Having heard about Jesus, she came up behind Him in the crowd and touched His clothing. For she said, "If I just touch His clothes, I'll be made well." Instantly her flow of blood ceased, and she sensed in her body that she was healed of her affliction. Immediately Jesus realized that power had gone out from Him. He turned around in the crowd and said, "Who touched my clothes?" His disciples said to Him, "You see the crowd pressing against you, and yet you say, 'Who touched me?'" But He was looking around to see who had done this. The woman, with fear and trembling, knowing what had happened to her, came and fell down before Him, and told Him the whole truth. "Daughter," He said to her, "your faith has saved you. Go in peace and be healed from your affliction."

I have always loved this story in Scripture. But now, it had so much more meaning to me. A woman had been bleeding for 12 years, and no doctor could help her. I had been bleeding—not for 12 years—but it felt like it many days. I had battled RA for almost 30 years and now was beginning life as an amputee. The woman knew about Jesus and wanted to not only see Him but also touch the hem of His garment to be healed.

As I pictured this scene in my mind, I was the woman. I would close my eyes and envision myself stretching forth, wanting to simply touch Jesus' garment. I would picture Him at my bedside, not saying a word, His presence giving me comfort. I wanted to touch Him and have Him make me whole again. But apart from the physical healing we see in Scripture, Jesus made the woman spiritually whole.

Notice Jesus started with her spiritual healing, not her physical healing. "Your faith has saved you. Go in peace and be healed from your affliction." The most important part was her faith and salvation. Her physical healing was simply secondary. As I pictured this scene over and over in my head, I so badly wanted physical healing. But that wasn't coming in the form of my leg regenerating. I believe God was showing me that my faith was of most importance. My belief in Him throughout all the heartache and trauma I faced was all I needed. He would take care of the rest.

At the time I had transferred to step-down, COVID was ramping up again, and I was limited to one visitor, which was Beth. The nurse manager knew my case and all I had been through and deemed Jaylynn "clergy," so she could also come. It would be the only time Jaylynn would be classified as a "pastor" in her life.

As I waited to be transferred to Baptist Rehab, I had PT sessions and continued working on eating a very soft diet. The food they brought was awful. I wasn't hungry and would rather just drink ginger ale. Jaylynn began to bring me Coke Icees. Those were like healing for my body! A Coke Icee is full of sugar, which I definitely needed, and was easy for me to swallow. I lived on Coke Icees and peanut butter for many days.

On January 11, I returned to Baptist Rehab. I didn't return full of glee to see my "family" again as I was battling the grief of why I was still here and the loss of my leg. I knew the intense regimen of rehab, and I couldn't foresee how I would endure therapy every day. As I was wheeled into my room, I had a big sign on the whiteboard "Welcome Back to Rehab." It should have brightened my spirits, but I was too downtrodden. I couldn't sit up and, because my core was decimated, I had difficulty carrying on a conversation. Many years ago, I took voice lessons. Those lessons taught me how to breathe from my diaphragm. Once I was trained in that way, it was my natural form of breathing. Now that my muscles were weak, even talking was hard.

The nurse who admitted me was Karen G. There were three Karens in the rehab unit, so all of them had to go by the initial of their last name. From my previous stays, I had never had Karen G. as a personal nurse, but boy, I knew her. She had this contagious laugh that wafted down the hallways of rehab, permeating the downtrodden souls that occupied every room. She knew me as well (since I was returning to my medical Cheers), but what I didn't know was the amazing bond we would make during this stay.

Breathlessly, I did my best to catch her up on all that had happened to me since I'd last left rehab in November. The rehab staff knew I was returning, and my name was on the "incoming" wall of patients, but some of them didn't know all the particulars of why I was so delayed. Needless to say, I lay there, hardly able to talk and thinking I would never be able to withstand this rigorous schedule. What would I do in rehab when I couldn't even sit up unassisted?

Once again, I had Laura and Connie as my PT and OT, respectively. I can't describe the feeling of relief to be back with people who knew me and whom I loved. The next day, I would begin my journey to my new life. I felt like I'd started this trek so many times before. I didn't know exactly how I would ever recover from all I'd been through, or how to believe that this could truly be the end of what felt like endless surgeries and rehab. My spirit of resiliency, mixed with my human frailty, was waging war inside. I had used up my Pollyanna mojo and didn't think I could return to the person I was before this health journey started. This recovery was going to be hard, and I couldn't muster up laughter and joy in my current state. I was still grieving. The fact was, my life would never be the same again, and as I grieved the loss of my leg, I had to grieve my former life as well.

My first therapy session was PT, and the fear of what this would entail had me shaking on the inside. Laura came to retrieve me, wheeling me in a "cardiac" chair. I'm not sure why this rolling contraption carried that name, but to me, it looked like a very large and cumbersome wheelchair. Great. Now I've regressed to some monster of a wheelchair. Laura came with help, so I knew this was step one of doing my therapy for the day.

The cardiac chair was used for patients who couldn't easily get into a regular wheelchair. <Raises hand> A life-sized board was used to transfer me from my bed to the chair. The chair would lay back completely flat for transfer, and then they would sit me upright. From there, I would be buckled in and taken to the rehab gym. I don't know that I've felt as helpless while completely coherent as I did at that moment. I was at the mercy of two, sometimes three, people to get me into the cardiac chair and then back in bed once I was done with therapy. I had no ability to sit up on my own. I couldn't imagine improving to a level where I could sit up independently, much less wear and walk in a prosthetic and live life.

The first day was very light as I did exercises in my cardiac chair and then a few on the mat. A village was required to help me transfer from the cardiac chair to the mat. Laura was so encouraging, cheering me on that I would improve. It would just take time. Time. Hadn't I already spent so much "time" on this journey? No one really gave a timeframe, which wasn't comforting when I felt I might not be functioning before the 2024 presidential election.

When PT was over, it was lunchtime, and I was exhausted. Being tired wasn't conducive to eating, and everyone already knew I wasn't crazy about eating. The food at rehab was the same as the hospital fare, except I was put on a soft diet, so everything looked mushy and the same color, no matter what was on the menu. I tried to stomach a few bites, but it was hard.

The afternoon involved more PT and OT with Connie. I spent the morning with her, getting cleaned up and dressed for the day. Given my current state, I had to do all of that in bed with a lot of assistance. Being tossed and tugged around made me feel like a rag doll. The afternoon session of OT involved weights to strengthen my upper body. I knew I was weak, but struggling to lift a one-pound weight proved I had lost so much muscle mass.

I was still on IV antibiotics, and Dr. Gormley stayed on top of all my blood work. While he did his initial rounds, he said to me, "I need you to eat as much as you can." Listen, we live for a doctor to tell us that, don't we? Even Dr. Sweet rounded on me, pointed to a bag of cookies on my table, and said, "You've got to eat everything…including that bag of cookies." I had begun to progress from soft to more solid foods, and the nurses had brought me those cookies to encourage my growth. In the past, I would have devoured them, but I couldn't get excited about them right now. My body was completely void of vitamins and nutrition. My protein level was abysmal. My iron was low. Combing my hair in the morning resulted in clumps of it coming out on the brush due to malnutrition and the amount of anesthesia I had in my body.

The problem was I didn't want to eat. This was partly because my stomach had shrunk from the weeks I hadn't eaten and partly because I really didn't have any motivation to eat. My mental state in rehab was in stage four of the grieving process—depression. If I was honest, I didn't want to be alive. I had faced death three times, and the last time I almost did leave this world. Dancing in the valley of the shadow of death made me long for eternity, long for what was beyond this world.

Simply put: I wanted to be with Jesus. I wanted to be with my parents. I had lived a decent life, and I couldn't understand why God would keep me here. I couldn't do anything for myself. What was the point?

This led to me feeling very separated from this world. Beth and Jaylynn were the only visitors allowed, and I'd put on a good face when they visited, but it wasn't what I was feeling. During this time, I would get word that someone I knew had passed away. My friend, Antoinette, lost her mom during this time. Her mom was 88 and had gone septic, much like I had done two times before, but she didn't survive. When I heard the news, my heart hurt for Antoinette, knowing how it felt to lose your mother. My thoughts went quickly to her mom — I longed to trade places with her mother. Why did God take her but not me? It wasn't just survivors' guilt. I had a feeling that I somehow missed my plane to Heaven, and I didn't want to wait to catch the next one...I needed a chartered flight to get me there now.

The nurses and aides were my lifeline. Karen G. was especially pivotal in my life. She hung up inspirational quotes and pictures all over my room to motivate me to keep going. I needed to get my head in the game to keep going, but I'd already played multiple overtimes in this game of life, and I didn't want the trophy. I was done. Another nurse, Mandy, brought me a sticker-by-number book to occupy my time. All the staff would take time to listen to me and encourage me, even though no one really knew how deeply sad I truly was. I think Karen G. knew how depressed I was, though. I would talk to her more than any other nurse, and she continued to keep me motivated.

Dr. Gormley encouraged me to eat a protein snack at all meals and bedtime. He also suggested I drink protein shakes. When he realized Baptist didn't have the protein shakes that were highest in protein, he bought me the same shakes I had at home after I came out of rehab the first time. What doctor does that!? When I came home after six months of rehab and hospitals in 2020, my PT friend, Jon, advised me to drink one protein shake a day to build up the muscle mass I had lost from being bedridden. I continued to drink them while I was home. From then on, Beth would keep me stocked, and the aides would get them for me when they brought my food. Once again, Karen G. came to the rescue. She brought me cans of Boyardee Spaghettios, chili, and every kind of protein snack you could think of. I had a bucket full of protein bars, trail mix, bags of nuts, beef jerky, and even Payday candy bars, since they had more protein than some protein bars.

Jaylynn and Beth would bring me food from the outside that I could eat. Initially, I couldn't even eat a full serving of macaroni and cheese from Chick-fil-A. The first day I did, Beth and I had a celebration! Laura, Jaylynn's daughter-in-law, couldn't stand the thought of me eating the horrid hospital food, so she would send very healthy dishes the aides could warm up for me to eat in lieu of my dinner. Laura is not only an excellent cook but makes extremely healthy dishes. She would just plate up a portion from their family's meal and send it with Jaylynn. Eating all of that food helped me to develop an appetite again.

Toward the end of January, I began to sit up on my own. What a victory! Despite this, I still struggled with sadness and depression. I wanted to be strong and respond in a positive way, but everything about this situation seemed hopeless. I was grieving the loss of my leg and the life I knew. There wasn't a silver lining to this black cloud that seemed to be securely fixed above my head. I didn't like who I was. Ever since I became a Christian, I had been a Pollyanna. I kept that positive attitude through the loss of loved ones, my undiagnosable health issues, job losses, the loss of my parents, and even the losses I had early on this journey. But I'd reached a point where I couldn't find my joy.

Closing my eyes, I would desperately want to talk to God, but I couldn't. I wasn't angry *at* Him; I was angry at what happened. I never blamed God for what had happened because I foundationally knew this happened for a reason, and I just didn't know what that reason was. But I couldn't pray. It was as if I'd forgotten how to pray. I had no words. During this time, I knew the prayers of all those in my life were doing that work for me. It was also when Romans 8:26 became so very real to me:

> In the same way the Spirit also helps us in our weakness, because we do not know what to pray for as we should, but the Spirit Himself intercedes for us with inexpressible groanings.

I had quoted that verse hundreds of times to people I served in ministry. I thought I truly believed and understood it, but it wasn't until I was unable to utter one word in prayer to my Father that it rang true in my heart. I knew God was with me; I just didn't know how to process all that I had been through and even talk about how I was feeling. To be honest,

I wasn't sure how I felt. I'd battled the enemy on this journey, but now I felt numb.

As a visual person, I began to visualize Jesus at my bedside. Or even sitting on a park bench with me. He would sit beside me, with His arm around me, but not saying a word. My heart wanted Him to gush out to me all that was going on in the unseen so I could grasp why all of this was happening. I would close my eyes and visualize this almost every day. When I did, it was a calming picture as I sat beside my Savior saying nothing and Him saying nothing back. He just had His arm around me. I knew He was there, and that was all I needed to know.

Aside from reclaiming my appetite and learning how to sit up independently, I had an incision that needed to heal. I so desperately wanted it to heal so I could be fitted for a prosthetic sooner than later. But alas, what would my story be if I had a wound that healed properly? Normal, that's what it would be, and I'm far from the norm.

Dr. Gormley called in Dr. Majzoub (pronounced "Ma-zoob") to take a look at me. He had seen me at the hospital prior to my amputation, as Dr. Sweet had called him in to try and heal my knee incision. He came and began a treatment on my incision that he hoped would encourage healing. My body wasn't on my side, as protein and good nutrition are critical for healing, and I wasn't where I needed to be.

After a week or so, Dr. Majzoub felt it was necessary to do a revision surgery. In the world of amputation, a revision procedure is often done to "clean up" an area after the initial amputation or possibly remove more of a limb, such as going from a below knee to an above knee. I had some areas of necrotic (dead) tissue that needed to be removed to allow healthy tissue to grow. I was told this was very common and that almost every amputee needs revision surgeries. Finally, something normal! Thankfully, I was able to stay in rehab and just be transported to surgery and then back to my rehab room. Unless there were some complications with the surgery, in which case I would be admitted to the hospital. I prayed there wouldn't be and that I could head back to rehab from post-op.

Surgery #13 occurred on January 27. It all went very well, and I was back to rehab in no time. The number 13 has always been lucky for me, so I'm not surprised that the 13th surgery was very uneventful. I was allowed to rest that day but headed back to the grind of rehab the day after surgery. The tyrants also known as therapists have to keep you moving forward. I even had to put in a full day on the weekend to make up for my surgery day.

I longed for my residual limb to heal after this surgery so that I wouldn't have any more setbacks. I was slowly beginning to come out of my depression, yet I couldn't pinpoint anything specific that caused me to turn a corner. I believe the earthly reasons I was turning a corner were my appetite returning, my progress in rehab, and my growing strength. But the real reason I was improving in such a way was due to a Savior who loves me so much He wasn't going to let me go. I wanted to let go. I was ready to leave this world, but God knew it wasn't time. God was so patient with me as I wrestled with all the emotions I was feeling, many emotions I didn't even understand. He knew there wouldn't be a way for my finite mind to grasp all He was doing in the background. So He smiled at me, with an arm around me on that park bench while He continued to love me through the highs and lows of this journey - even though I couldn't understand why.

Chapter Thirty

February 2022 - March 2022

· • ◉ • ·

A s I continued working hard in rehab, the endorphins that were released helped uplift my spirits. I continued to struggle with my grief and emotions, trying to grasp all I'd been through and what was to come. Sometimes I would be in bed, look down, and realize my leg was gone. Like it was some new reality that had just occurred. Would I ever find myself not gasping over my missing limb? I so desperately wanted to but didn't know how.

Karen G. continued to be the nurse who was always there to listen to my continued rambles about all that was going on with me. I discovered that after 26 months, I developed what I called the "fainting goat syndrome." Have you ever seen fainting goats? They're a species of goats that have a startle reflex that causes them to literally faint at the slightest noise. That was me…I was the fainting goat. The moment someone would share anything that wasn't completely positive, I freaked. And although I didn't fall over to the ground, my reaction was similar in emotion. Although I'd like to point out that with one leg, it's a lot easier to fall over.

One day, while I was talking to Karen G., she mentioned a cartoon she'd seen that summed up our lives as humans quite well. It was a picture of a caterpillar and a butterfly enjoying a beverage together. The caterpillar's cartoon bubble says, "You've changed," and the butterfly's bubble says, "We're supposed to." I loved that so much. Karen G. printed off a copy and hung it on my wall amidst the rest of the encouraging quotes that she'd adorned after my arrival.

Valentine's Day was coming soon. Karen G. decorated my walls with hearts, cupids, and other flashy decorations so I'd feel loved during this holiday time. Spending holidays in the hospital or rehab was the norm for me, and this holiday was no exception. Frankly, it would have been odd to experience any holiday in my home and not in the hospital or rehab. I knew the time was coming when I would leave rehab, but I was concerned about going home too soon.

My residual limb was still not healing completely. It definitely looked better than it did before the last surgery, but Dr. Gormley and Dr. Majzoub seemed concerned. After a week or so, Dr. Majzoub said he wanted to do another surgery to clean things up a bit more to allow for healing. Nooooo! I felt like some test dummy for operating rooms. I knew it was for the best, but to say I was growing weary of surgeries was an understatement. On February 24, surgery was set. Surgery #14, here we come.

Like the previous surgery, I was allowed to return to rehab right after post-op, which helped soften the blow of the procedure. The surgery went well, and Dr. Majzoub was very positive that this would do the trick to heal my leg. I wanted to heal soon so I could start the prosthetic process. Until my residual limb was healed, the prosthetists couldn't take measurements to make my leg. I knew walking was my goal, and I needed a prosthetic to accomplish that task. It was as if I saw walking as the moment I would arrive. Or maybe it was to prove others wrong, like Dr. Yakanti, who said most above-knee amputees never walk again. When I hear "no," I am competitive enough to make it a "yes."

Unlike 2020 Rose, I wasn't the same obsessive gal trying to get back to my old life. My old life was gone, and I was working through emotions about the loss of my leg and the loss of my life as I knew it. I remembered my prayer of surrender in October, and I knew God had His best for me. But emotionally and spiritually, I just couldn't see past the present circumstances to find comfort in that. I was human, and we're sinful and selfish. Sure, I knew this was part of God's plan. But like a kid who thinks their plan is better than their parents', I was in a mode of trying to accept my path, and it was not for the faint of heart. Reflecting back, had I not prayed that prayer in October, I believe I would have been even lower. There is freedom in surrender. When we surrender to Jesus, we are freed from our sins. It might have been hard to surrender my will to God, but I knew it would be the best way. I just needed my heart to come along on this ride of surrender.

I was learning to transfer from the bed to my wheelchair and to the mats in the rehab gym. The first time I tried to stand up to pivot, there were three or four additional people assisting me. As I stood up, I was made aware I didn't have a right leg. Out of muscle memory and habit, I attempted to push my right foot down to stand. I'll never forget that feeling—it was one of the most direct reminders that I had lost my leg.

My emotional struggle became an obsession for me. I would fixate on people walking, admiring their two legs, wishing I'd done more when I had both my legs. I would get frustrated with people on television or social media who clearly lived life as free-spirited as it gets. My stages of grief were out of order, but they were there. Anger was hitting me in an uncommon way. I was angry that people who had no reverence for the Lord, or any thought of how great they had it with two legs, had a much easier life than me. The anger felt like the scene in *Steel Magnolias* when M'Lynn is at the gravesite of her daughter, Shelby, trying to make sense of Shelby's life being cut so short. M'Lynn screaming, "I just want to hit somebody until they feel as bad as I do!" summed up how I felt deep inside. I had served the Lord since I became a Christian. Sure, I still sinned, but I did my best to follow God. Yet, here I was without my leg. I didn't have two good legs before my amputation, and now I was even more hindered. I struggled to understand how I could live for the Lord and still end up in this place. I wrestled with this new emotion, knowing I could do nothing about it but let it fester inside me or give it over to the Lord.

I'm good at internalizing things to the point where I can't pray about it without rolling it over in my mind. The end of 2 Corinthians 10:5 says,

"We take every thought captive to obey Christ." I would dwell on these thoughts, begin to get angry, and then do my best to rein them in before I let them take control of me. I knew if I didn't rein in my thoughts, my anger would fester, and I would lash out verbally at someone. It's not anyone's fault that they have two legs and I don't. I had to deal with this internal anger to get it under control. The idea of taking a thought captive never became so clear to me than in this season of life. I knew what I needed to do but was fighting with myself constantly.

"You've tried to live an obedient life, and look what it got you."

"The Lord won't leave you, and He has a plan for you."

"I don't care what kind of plan He has; it can't be as good as what I could do with both legs."

"You have to trust in God, even when it doesn't make sense."

These thoughts would ruminate through me night and day. Then, I would remind myself of three statements that had been my go-to phrase for the past two-and-a-half years: "God is always faithful. He is always good. And He is always right." Three things I needed to be reminded of regularly. In fact, as I kept people informed of what was going on via social media posts, every post ended with that same phrase, followed by *Soli Deo gloria.*

Soli Deo gloria is the Latin term for "glory to God alone." It was significant to me because Jan, my little "sister" from Trinidad, always signed every card to me with that statement. If you recall, I longed to be with Jan during my first dance in the valley when I thought I was going to die. Repeating that phrase reminded me of her, but it also reminded me of a God who deserves all the glory in every situation I encounter. Whether good or bad, I wanted to be sure I glorified God. Jan taught me that long ago.

Finally, one day my anger was overcome with a realization from the Holy Spirit. I felt the Spirit say to me, "Rose, the party isn't here." I had forgotten how short our life here on Earth will be. Oh sure, we feel like this is a long time, and it's all we know in a tangible sense. But one day, we'll all leave this world for another one. Because I believed Jesus was my

Savior, I had the assurance of spending eternity with Him. I don't know what that looks like or what to expect, but the Bible teaches us that it is far beyond what we can grasp. And though many people with both legs are having a party here, throwing all caution to the wind and seemingly getting by with little to no tragedy, if they don't follow Christ, there will come a day when the party stops. When that happens and their eternity is spent separated from God, they won't care whether they had two legs or not; their misery will be for eternity. Alternatively, spending eternity with God will be a never-ending party where I'll dance with two legs better than I ever danced on Earth. Let's be honest. I never was the best dancer.

I had dealt with denial when I was told I would lose my leg. I skipped anger and bargaining and went straight to depression. Bargaining never entered the equation because I never saw negotiation as an option. Anger came after my amputation as the reality of what happened began to sink in. When I wrestled through the anger with depression still looming, it was good to have the Holy Spirit speaking to me to jolt me into place. Once I realized the party wasn't here, I began my journey to acceptance.

One of the things Jaylynn advised was equipping my house for accessibility. This had been an ongoing conversation since I was told I would lose my leg. Jaylynn is more of a handyman than most men. She can do just about any home repair needed, and thoroughly enjoys it. As my project manager at home, she had Jon and Philip, our college and singles pastor, join her to do a walkthrough of my house. They discussed what needed to change, and then we devised a plan for renovations.

When I moved into my home in 2001 with my dad after my mom's passing, my dad made sure the house was wheelchair accessible through doorways and in other areas. Adapting my house was much easier than I first thought because it was made to accommodate wheelchairs. Jon advised adding certain things in the bathroom to assist with showering, such as other grab bars and the installation of a new shower head so I could easily bathe in the seated position. Jon and his wife, Ashley, had an extra microwave in their basement that they would donate so I could have a microwave at my level since my current one was located over the stove. Philip would build a ramp out of my house to the garage to allow for easy entry and exit. So many of these everyday tasks would suddenly become more difficult as an amputee - and possibly impossible - until I got a prosthetic if we didn't make some major changes.

The biggest change that was needed was new flooring. I had carpet throughout my entire house except for the kitchen and bathrooms, and the kitchen flooring was due for an overhaul. That was on my "to-do" list of house projects when I initially got sick. Jaylynn was able to recommend someone she trusted to lay laminate flooring in my kitchen, dining room, and master bedroom. These are the main areas where I would spend my time, and the laminate would be easier to care for and tremendously easier for me to navigate in my wheelchair. Thinking about all that needed to be done for this laminate to be installed was overwhelming. But, I knew that rolling on the carpet would be horrible on my arms, and I needed to get around my house easily. Having to make these adaptations made all of this very real and was a motivator toward acceptance. Jaylynn brought floor samples to rehab so I could choose the material, and my house was prepped.

You really don't know how much a church family truly means until you see them in action on your behalf. My house had to be packed up and moved for the flooring to be laid. The ladies in my BFG came and did all that, putting things in every available nook and cranny in the remainder of the house. Philip brought in a crew of single guys who moved all the big furniture into the garage and other available space. Even the bathroom served as a storage area for bureaus and desks.

Once the work was completed, Philip brought his guys over again to help place everything back from whence it came, and the BFG ladies returned to assemble my house. Things were cleaned out and put away, and what didn't have a "home" was stashed in my patio room and office for sorting and disposing later. As a Type A organizer, my stomach churned, wondering about the state I would find everything. But I was so grateful for those who helped transform my house and that I would be going back to the home I loved, and worrying about where things were placed seemed insignificant.

March came and I was getting stronger and knew my homecoming was nearing. I was nervous but ready to return after five months of incarceration in the hospital and rehab. COVID restrictions were slightly lifted, allowing other people to visit me. That made all the difference in my days. I so loved Beth and Jaylynn but craved being with my church family. The various pastors on staff would come, and it was a joy to visit with people again. Never take for granted the simple things in life—even a visit with a face you have barely seen in years.

As discharge day approached, I was extremely nervous. I knew Paige would be home with me for the first week or so, but how would I do life without someone helping me? I was going home without a limb, wheelchair-bound, and still fairly weak. I chuckled to myself how I was whining about using a walker almost two years prior. Now, I'd have to use a wheelchair for the foreseeable future as my right leg healed and I waited for my prosthetic fitting.

One of the things my social worker, Susan, thought would be beneficial was a home visit. Prior to COVID, these visits were common. The therapy team assigned to a patient would go to their home a week or two before discharge and figure out how they'd navigate within their home. It's one thing to learn how to do things in rehab and another thing to actually do them at home. Susan wasn't sure if the visit would be approved, but she would bring it up to Dr. Gormley, and we would see.

As the Lord would have it, I was approved for a home visit! I couldn't be happier. First, I would not be going home blindly but would have Laura and Connie there to help me figure out what I needed to work on in rehab before discharge. Second, I was going home. I hadn't seen my home since October. As scared as I was, this opportunity removed the fear because we were going to do a "dry run" as if I was home.

The day came for the visit, and I was nervous and thrilled all at the same time. We got home, and Laura got me into the house since the ramp wasn't completed yet. I rolled in and saw the flooring for the first time and…my home. My home. I was speechless. I think I was so over-whelmed that I couldn't cry, but down inside my heart, I was weeping. What a beautiful picture of love before me. Seeing my home was a pro-found moment for me as I witnessed how the hands of people who loved me unconditionally had transformed my space. I felt so undeserving, and the ability to somehow thank them became insurmountable. I knew I'd never be able to repay or thank everyone sufficiently for all the love I'd been shown the past two-and-a-half years. That's what God's love looks like. He loved me enough to send His Son to die for my sins, and there will never be enough ways I can thank Him, nor repay Him, for the debt of my sin.

We worked on transfers to the bed, recliner, and bathroom and deter-mined areas where we needed to adapt the situation at home and what to focus on in rehab. The visit was wonderful, and when it was time to leave, part of me didn't want to go. Not only did this visit stir up emotions over the love I had received from the countless people in my church family, it also reassured me that going home wasn't as scary as I thought. Maybe I could actually survive without a leg.

Heading back to rehab, I felt refreshed and some of my fears were relieved. I was ready to go back and focus on areas where I needed the most improvement. The nurses and aides asked me how it felt returning home. As I shared, I felt a slight bit of sadness and detected the same from them. These were my people. They had seen me through the darkest of my days. Leaving them wouldn't be easy, and I sensed they felt similarly. That didn't stop our celebrating that I was one step closer to breaking out of rehab.

My discharge date was set for March 23, a little more than five months since I stepped foot on this hospital campus. I came with two legs and a surrendered heart. I was leaving with one leg and a heart surrendered to the Lord, on its way to becoming more transformed than in my wildest dreams. During those five months, I went from hopeful to clinging on to the edge of the pit to falling in again. Throughout the almost two-and-a-half months of post-amputation rehab, I had found my way out of the pit once again. I would be leaving with a peace that wasn't understandable apart from the work of the Holy Spirit in my heart. I didn't realize all the ways God had changed me, but in the months to come, I would realize how He was changing me. My body wasn't the only thing that had made a drastic change. God was and is changing my heart.

My incision from the recent revision surgery still had not healed up, so departing from rehab meant I would have to visit Dr. Majzoub in his office. Home health was set up so I could have therapy at home and nursing visits to monitor my healing. I knew this drill all too well and was ready for the next steps. My fear had turned to bittersweet sadness as I would soon leave behind my rehab family. I didn't want to say goodbye because I felt like they had become part of me these past two months. Not being awakened by an aide to eat breakfast at 7:00 am, hearing my OT team coming to get me up and ready for a day of therapy or hearing Karen G.'s laughter as she approached my room seemed incomprehensible. Life would be changing again, and I prayed it would change all for the better.

The night before I was discharged, Andrea, one of my favorite night nurses, had planned a celebration. She brought cupcakes and a sweet card signed by the night shift staff. Andrea had been one of my cheerleaders, sharing stories of others and how they had succeeded as an amputee. I eventually met one of those success stories, and we have bonded since. I would miss these folks so much as they were there to make sure I slept well every night, was properly medicated, and continued on my healing journey.

On the day of discharge, I was ready, except for parting from the rehab staff. The day shift nurses had gotten me a coffee mug full of candy—they were determined to fatten me up somehow—and some body lotion and spray, along with a card that I cherish to this day. I couldn't believe I was heading home. Was I ready for this?

I felt a bit like Julie Andrews' character, Maria, in *The Sound of Music*. I had changed from a Pollyanna to a Maria—scared of what was to come but marching forward with confidence and all the optimism I could muster. Maria left the Abbey and headed to the Von Trapp home with a heart full of wonder and fear of the unknown. She took a deep breath, stepped off the bus that took her near her destination, and then danced her way to the gates of the Von Trapp estate singing, "I Have Confidence":

What will this day be like?
I wonder
What will my future be?
I wonder
It could be so exciting
To be out in the world
To be free

My heart should be wildly rejoicing
Oh, what's the matter with me?

I've always longed for adventure
To do the things I've never dared
Now here I'm facing adventure
Then why am I so scared?

Her lyrics echoed my emotions surrounding that day. I didn't know what the day or future held for me, but I knew I was walking (figuratively) into freedom. Part of my heart was staying with those who cared for me, and though I should have been rejoicing about my release following five months in the hospital and rehab, I was scared. Why? It was freedom, but would it come with a footnote? Was something around the corner that would bring me back here again? I left for my home cautiously optimistic.

As I rode away, looking at the rehab unit and my angel staff in the rearview mirror, my mind was everywhere, but I was heading home to begin the rest of my life. The car was loaded up with the few belongings

I had needed during the past five months, and I was on my way home to begin my life as an amputee. And, with apologies to Richard Rogers, here is my rewritten version of the first chorus:

So let the world bring all their problems
I'll do better than my best
I have confidence
They'll put me to the test
But I'll beat the odds
I have confidence in God

Epilogue

· • ● • ·

T here really isn't a way to put an ending to this story. As I write these words a little over a year from when I left rehab, my journey is far from over. But, isn't that what everyone's life is like? We weave in and out of different seasons without knowing what tomorrow holds. My fully-surrendered heart left rehab that day with a peace that whatever would come my way, the Lord would see me through.

I spent the next five months waiting for my incision to heal. It was quite the trigger as I kept anticipating my home health nurse to wave the flag that infection was present. After multiple visits to the wound doctor, I was finally released to be fitted for my prosthetic in September! The process took a few weeks, but when I wore it for the first time, I experienced the feeling that maybe I would walk again. My first steps came almost exactly a year from the last time I took steps. Thankfully, my home PT had been conditioning me in preparation for this moment. As I write these words, I am walking in my home with a walker and learning to increase my time each day. Soon, I will tackle walking outside in the community. Look out, world!

Outpatient rehab began twice a week in the same gym I left in March 2022. Each visit to rehab allowed me to reconnect with those sweet care-givers that saw me at my very lowest. I nominated Karen G. for the Daisy Award, which honors nurses who have provided excellent care. The process is long, and very few nominees win the award, as a stringent panel of judges make the decision. But, as the Lord would have it, she won! I was able to be present for the presentation and couldn't have been happier to see her be recognized in such an honorable way. Laura, my PT, decided to retire in autumn 2022 after an illness. I was thrilled to be able to be at her retirement party—thanks to the outpatient staff who made sure she didn't know I was coming. Connie is still rocking the OT world and was promoted to lead OT, such a well-deserved promotion.

Dr. Sweet is still killing the orthopedic game. His dad retired recently, and he carries on his legacy for what I hope will be years to come. In 2022, Dr. Sweet became a father, himself, of a precious daughter, Charlotte. I hope she follows in her daddy's footsteps and joins the world of orthopedics.

Beth "retired" from her position at our church as preschool director during my health journey to focus on caring for her new grandbaby, Rowyn, look after Beth's mom, and to help me. She is busier than ever before, and this "Mimi" will have grandbaby number two in December 2023.

Paige has been able to enjoy visits with me without being my caregiver. I look forward to the day I can travel to Alabama again to visit her and her husband, Steve, and their lovable dogs.

Jaylynn continues to be a huge support for me. Almost every Tuesday, she takes me to rehab, cleans my floors and bathrooms, and helps with laundry. The time we spend together is invaluable to me as we discuss ministry and our personal lives. I love our time, and I hope it is as therapeutic for her as it is for me.

My friends, Christie and Chad, still come one night during the week for dinner, even though I'm capable of making food for myself. I treasure these times because I don't take time with friends for granted. Living alone, I cherish people spending time with me. COVID and my rehab imprisonment have made me crave time with people.

My friend, Heather, who I'll mention more later, was a part of this journey in the background. We co-teach our BFG with our friend, Lindsey, and we've grown much closer through this time. That all started from her pre-COVID rehab visits and continues with our weekly Saturday night sessions.

My friends, Dana and Janet, come during the week to help with things I can't do yet—like picking up my grocery order, helping with my laundry, and doing other chores around the house. I love my time with each of them, and the support they give me is tremendous and has also allowed our friendship to grow.

My friend, Karen, spent every Sunday after church with me but recently moved to Danville, Kentucky. She has equipped my wardrobe with dresses and tops from her expert thrifting. I didn't have many dresses, and in the beginning, those were the easiest to wear to function throughout my day. Thanks to her, I now have a closet full of fashionable choices!

The outpatient rehab team has been phenomenal, and after ten months of rehab, I have "graduated" for now. This process is a long one. As an above-knee amputee, learning to walk is more of a challenge than a below-knee amputee. I have to learn to walk, balance, and operate a knee joint that isn't mine. Along with my RA and the recovery I needed to rebuild from almost three years of being incapacitated, I realize there is still a lot of work to be done. I believe no one wanted to break that news to me when I started the amputee journey, as I'd already been on a very long road. However, I am still on the road and have good and bad days. Some days, I feel like I haven't progressed at all. Or I get really fatigued from trying to do too much and wonder if I'll ever be able to do more than I can right now. But, when I make a breakthrough and walk further, or begin to learn how to walk an incline, I realize I am progressing after all. Remember how long it takes a toddler to learn how to walk? That's where I am, and I'm doing it all on a leg that isn't mine. The advantage for toddlers is they have less farther to fall and are walking on a God-created leg. This journey of rehab and learning to walk all over again feels somewhat like CrossFit on steroids. But, I haven't found myself in that pit or dancing in the valley, and for that, I am grateful.

As of this writing, my next step post-rehab is to continue walking until I feel more stable and then progress to walking outside my home. In the meantime, I'm working on getting approved for a power wheelchair. Given my RA, to regain my independence the quickest, getting a power wheel-chair is the goal. It won't stop me from continuing to walk and get stronger, but it will allow me the independence I've prayed for so long. From there, I hope to get a minivan customized to allow me to go out with my power wheelchair and drive myself wherever I want to go. Words can't express how elated I feel at the prospect of being fully independent to go places!

Personally, I launched a podcast with my friend, Heather, called *One Single Thought*. It has been one of my greatest joys since coming out of rehab. I would be amiss if I didn't also mention that just a few months after my amputation, I completed a writing cohort with Joy Eggerichs Reed (which I had put off for a year after my initial acceptance) that allowed me to build a book proposal, write the story you have just read, and start the path that made me a Punchline Publishers author. The journey to that cohort is a book in itself, but suffice it to say God made a way.

Many people ask me where God is directing me next. I have no answer to that question. I haven't returned to full-time work as of yet, and I'm not sure if or when I ever will. For now, I'm continuing to sur-render to Him. He led me to write this book. He led me to start a pod-cast. And I'm doing more and more ministry with my church amidst my recovery. Reading those few sentences reminds me of what I now say so often: *It is possible that God is making all my dreams come true through the circumstances of the worst time of my life.* That's the type of God He is.

As a girl, I had to learn to do childhood differently, often observ-ing others and cheering them on as they did the activities I couldn't due to my JRA pain. Throughout my young adulthood, although I pressed on through the pain to live my life as normal as possible, my childhood taught me how to overcome when I was faced with a challenge that would physically hold me back. Now, as an amputee, I am learning that my life has been a training ground for today. Being an amputee is all about learning to adapt your life to live it to the fullest. This road isn't easy, but learning to adapt isn't a new phenomenon for me.

There are so many lessons I'm still learning. I'm learning that life can go on with only one leg. Don't sweat the small things because life is too short. You can't take anything with you when you die...but your friends. Share Jesus with them while you can. And the wise words that Linus Van Pelt said to Charlie Brown after he lost the spelling bee, "Did you notice something, Charlie Brown? The world didn't come to an end." But, the three most important lessons still remain. I pray that I'll never forget them, no matter where the road takes me. God is faithful. God is good. And, God is always right.

I want to close with a verse that has become so dear to me. Psalm 139:16 says:

> Your eyes saw me when I was formless; all my days were written
> in your book and planned before a single one of them began.

Long before I even had a form, God saw me. He opened up His book to the page titled "Rose Booth," and He wrote out every day perfectly as they would happen. His pen elegantly crafted a life no one could believe and I could never fathom. I call myself an author now, but the writing of this book, or any other book I may pen, will never come close to the story God wrote for me. You see, He isn't *writing* my story. The story is already *written*. I'm just living it out. And He's done the same for you. There is no greater Author than God.

As you close this book, I pray that you leave with a new or renewed faith in our Lord and Savior, Jesus Christ. I want you to take with you the joy I have found in Him. Through all the days of wrestling with my faith, He was faithful. This Christian Pollyanna had to learn to trust through the valleys. On the other side, I see how I danced in the valley while God revealed His plan for me. It wasn't the plan I had mapped out, but it was choreographed to be better than I could ever hope for. And, I can say that I'd rather follow Jesus with one leg than to live with both legs and be without Him.

Soli Deo gloria.

About the Author

·•◉•·

Rose Booth hails from Louisville, Kentucky, where she was born and raised. As an only child to older parents, she was encouraged to be an independent soul. This has served her well as a single, never-married woman living to serve Christ.

Rose has worked for more than thirty years in the technology and publishing space. She received her MBA in 2015, and thrives in environments where she can mentor and counsel others to grow in their careers and personal lives.

Rose co-directs the women's ministry at her church, Ninth & O Baptist, in Louisville, Kentucky, and also co-teaches her ladies' Bible study class. Her passion in ministry is teaching and discipleship, and she loves working with women from college age and above. Rose co-hosts a podcast, *One Single Thought*, with her friend, Heather Bump.

Becoming an amputee in December 2021 has caused Rose to see life from a different perspective as she learns to navigate this new normal.

When she's not writing, Rose loves to spend time with friends, craft, volunteer, and read. She also loves shocking people with the news that she is a distant relative of John Wilkes Booth.

Acknowledgments

· •●• ·

I t is nearly impossible to acknowledge everyone who has played a part in this, my first book. If you read the entire book, thank you. Within these pages, I've mentioned many people who had an impact on my life, specifically in the most recent health journey that launched me into writing my story. So here is my feeble attempt at making sure I recognize those on this journey.

First off, I have to thank Joy Eggerichs Reed, founder of Punchline Agency and the mastermind of Punchline Publishers. After three attempts at trying to do her writing cohort (and Joy thinking, "This girl can't be telling the truth. I think she's catfishing me."), I finally was able to do it, and it changed my life. Joy helped make my dreams come true.

Amelia Graves helped make these pages come alive by challenging me to bring out my emotions and vividly describe the events of my life. Her editorial skills are unrivaled. My copyeditor, Stephanie Foertsch, made sure my grammatical skills and form were exceptional, even while she was traveling across the globe. My cover artist, Clayton Roederer, is so dear to my heart. He is my adopted nephew, and when I thought of what I wanted on my cover, a piece that he illustrated popped into my head. He was able to take my theme and turn it into what everyone sees first when searching for my book. Asya Blue made the inside and outside of my book fit the personality and vibe of my story. She is so effortlessly talented, and I'm grateful I found her.

Ninth & O Baptist Church is not only my church home but also my family. I can't begin to thank each person at that church for what they have meant on this journey. As a third-generation member, it was because of this church that I followed Christ and that I'm serving Him daily. It was because of this church that I traveled the hardest journey of my life with unbelievable love and support. The fragrant aroma of this church is merely a whiff of what it will be like in the presence of my Savior.

I have countless friends who have been by my side in the most difficult of times, and I mentioned them on the pages of this book. Every name that was mentioned has my heart and made an impact on me and my story. Recounting them here seems redundant if you've read their stories on the pages of my book. I would not want to do life without these friends who held me up when I was struggling to navigate the valley.

I am forever grateful to my mom and dad. They never gave up so that I would have life. Without them, there would be no story to write. They taught me how to love Jesus and follow Him, even in death. With each passing day, I realize their example shaped me into who I am today. Though my time with them on earth was so much shorter than I had hoped, their legacy lives on through my life. I cannot wait to spend eternity with them.

Lastly, I thank my Lord and Savior, Jesus Christ. It seems so pithy to say "thank you" to the very One who gave me breath and who sustains me each and every day. My story is His story. He wrote it long before I was formed. May I live each day to give Him the praise.

God is faithful. God is good. And, God is always right. Soli Deo gloria.

Printed in the USA
CPSIA information can be obtained
at www.ICGtesting.com
LVHW010846081223
765818LV00074B/2117